WILD WOMEN DON'T WEAR NO BLUES

W ILD W OMEN

DON'T WEAR NO BLUES

DOUBLEDAY

NEW YORK LONDON TORONTO SYDNEY AUCKLAND

Black Women Writers

on Love

Men

and Sex

EDITED AND WITH AN INTRODUCTION BY

MARITA GOLDEN

PUBLISHED BY DOUBLEDAY
a division of Bantam Doubleday Dell Publishing Group, Inc.
1540 Broadway, New York, New York 10036

DOUBLEDAY and the portrayal of an anchor with
a dolphin are trademarks of Doubleday,
a division of Bantam Doubleday Dell
Publishing Group, Inc.

Acknowledgments for individual works appear on pages 231–32.

Book design by Terry Karydes

Library of Congress Cataloging-in-Publication Data
Wild women don't wear no blues :
Black women writers on love, men, and sex /
edited and with an introduction by Marita Golden. — 1st ed.
p.   cm.
1. Afro-American women authors—20th century—Attitudes.
2. Man-woman relationships—United States.
3. Afro-Americans—Sexual behavior.
4. Love.   I. Golden, Marita.
PS153.N5W46   1992
814'.540809287—dc20   92-21188
CIP

ISBN 0-385-42400-0
Copyright © 1993 by Marita Golden

All Rights Reserved
Printed in the United States of America
August 1993

3   5   7   9   10   8   6   4   2

To the memory of Audre Lorde,

force of nature and of life,

sexual rebel,

natural woman,

and HUMAN BEING par excellence

DA

Editor's Acknowledgments

Thanks to the writers who made this project easier than i imagined, more fun than i thought possible, and an education i didn't expect. They are professionals, conjurers, and blessed "wild women" all.

Thanks too, to Martha Levin, a wonderful editor, who helped us all to bring this baby home.

Contents

What happens when you ask a Black woman to think, not in passing, but long and hard, about love, men, and sex? At first, there are no words, but rather, a sudden rush, a cacophonous internal revolt of feelings pressing for release but strangely mute. What to say when you've never been asked? What to say when you've been written off too often, as dangerous, irrelevant, not to be trusted? At first, there is silence. Not because there is nothing to say but because there is too much, never asked, never sought or listened to.

As a Black girl, no matter your class or your complexion (invisible but enduring dividing lines), you knew there were no Prince Charmings in your neighborhood. The few Black men who had any REAL money had earned it the old-fashioned way, and had not been bequeathed it through the genes. And, you like to think that if you'd been Cinderella, you'd have hightailed it away from that positively weird step-mutha long before that shoe business. You like to think that. But would you? Could you have? Being Black ensures there will be struggle; it doesn't guarantee the tools to fight back. One myth down. Three thousand to go.

So, if there were no fairy tales, could there be love? Society has so melded the two, it's impossible to tell the difference. And what KIND of love? Where would you take your cues? From the songs on the radio that urged women to be slaves and men to be fools? Perhaps you would breathe in, like air, the potent yet subtle belief among many of the women you knew that "A Black man can't be trusted." Remember, WE couldn't be trusted either. Love was a word used ad nauseam on TV, in the movies, in books. But what was it and where would you learn what it portended for you? The breathless, weighty sound of the word, being embraced or denied, hinted that it was as potentially dangerous as a weapon or a drug. Few of the adults around you talked much about love, consigning it, when you asked, to that never-never-land of "When you grow up."

Still, you suspected that much of the flight from talking about love—even while the culture's deepest fantasies were muddled by corruptions of it—had something to do with the requirement of your people to be vigilant, protecting the crumbs swept their way by a nation feasting on broken promises. You were young, but instinctively, you knew all this somehow shaped the KIND of love a people develops.

If you fight your way through this emotional morass to approach the discussion of love, the prospect of dissecting sex may drain you of speech. Other people's racism, and guilt, distorted a sexuality you have never until now been able to call your own. In a twisted response, Black men, and women, too, often internalized the myth of sexual potency that required us to be whatever white men said we were. Still, while the stereotypes trapped everyone in a noose, determining each move, no one ever really, openly talked about sex. If they did, it was to recharge the lies. The assertion that "white men can't screw" (or run fast, or *really* play basketball, or sing or dance . . .) implies of necessity and by the illogic of racism that "That's ALL Black men CAN do." And you knew, living, breathing inside the hearts of some of your men (it SEEMED always the "best and brightest") lay the desire for the white woman, more tangible, more blessed even in dream than you.

Folklore was part of it too. You were told there were certain crimes, horrible, woman-hating crimes, no Black man could commit, for "crazy white men" were the real ones to fear. Play this deception in reverse, substitute white for Black. Sound familiar? You were told this over and over. This is what they told you about sex.

Of course, in order to have sex you had to be in love. Although you weren't certain what that was, you knew how it FELT. Love was the permission slip women required to have sex, otherwise you risked being a "bad girl," i.e., any woman who used her sexuality when and where and how she wanted to. SO, you were perpetually in love. When you tried to talk about sex the conversation, whether with men, other women, or yourself, was a verbal/emotional maze fraught with more heat than light.

And what were you talking about when you talked about men? Talking about men made it suddenly possible and safe to talk about love and sex. We didn't know it then, but when we talk about men we are talking about power and powerlessness, about choices, fears, limits and boundaries. We are even talking about ourselves when we think we're just talking about THEM. For we choose, when we choose a man, a psychic mirror we are sometimes afraid to look into.

It is impossible to talk about men without referencing our fathers, our mothers, and ourselves. WE can't talk to men unless with their help, language becomes a bridge rather than a barrier.

The current Pandora's box of revelations about sexual crimes committed within the walls of so many of America's families reveals the nuclear family to be cruelly, aptly named. Patriarchy, sexism, and the culture of capitalism have created a "family" that too often is no more than a ticking time bomb waiting to explode.

An archaeologist in the year 3050 could unearth MTV videos, beer commercials, tapes of our jokes about women, figures on sexual crimes and women in positions of power and know everything essential about how men and women lived in the twentieth century, an epoch that would appear then, I would hope, to be a very primitive age.

Yet, as the essays that follow attest, all is not lost, it never has been. We find and realize love. It is hard but possible. Marriage can be an act of courage and a source of eternal surprise, a well-spring of growth. Remaining single is an affirmation of self. And we don't have to use all the psychological baggage we inherit. We can empty our suitcases and repack them with new rules and possibilities.

And if color, as W. E. B. Du Bois prophetically predicted, was the dominant question of the twentieth century, then all the evidence points to sex becoming the defining metaphor for the century about to unfold. Sex and its myriad ramifications—from AIDS, abortion, birth control, sexual abuse, sexual orientation and rights, to women in all countries and cultures controlling the integrity of their bodies, challenging obsolete concepts of manhood and womanhood, infusing love with equality—will haunt our global and individual dialogues. Conscious, wide-awake women have always known that just as everything is political, so everything is sexual. That is the dirty little secret well-bred women never discussed until we started chiseling out a vocabulary that would accurately name and define our experience.

Naming and defining have provided the internal propulsion of the sexual revolution in which African-American women have been generals, field commanders, and foot soldiers. This still-in-progress revolution, like all challenges to the status quo, exists under siege. That is the only thing that we can count on.

There has been a revolution, despite the depressing statistics that chart the unstable course of female progress. Now we have names for the miseries once assumed to be inevitable crosses women were born to bear. Sexual abuse. Sexual harassment. Spousal rape. Battering. We've created new designations to name old terrors. And we use them. Using them alters reality and our sense of ourselves. We have new words. And we no longer shrink from the old ones. Rape. Incest. Once, women who loved women were "bulldaggers," "dykes." Now we know they are women who love women, nothing more, nothing less.

The women in this collection have found a way to speak, to break the code of silence women once had to honor in order to be loved, respected. These essays reject the notion that women conspire in their own victimization. These pieces meditate on love, sex, and men in the widest possible way, expanding, re-shaping, resuscitating the conventional wisdom. So often, Afri-can-American women write in reaction to the latest, most blatant outrage against our integrity. HERE, we are talking to ourselves, among ourselves, like if WE could write the story the way it's SUPPOSED to be, this is how it would sound. . . .

WILD WOMEN DON'T WEAR NO BLUES

Tough Boyz and Trouble:

Those Girls Waiting

Outside D.C. Jail

Remind Me of Myself

PATRICE GAINES

"**W**hen you're a black child who believes she has no control over her life, you create your own definition of freedom," Patrice Gaines observes of her adolescent and teenage fascination with "tough boys."

When you are a woman who believes she has no control over her heart, you create definitions of love as dangerous as the weapons "tough boys" carry. Gaines recalls with impassioned, poignant hindsight the skewed meanings of manhood, courage, and responsibility that once determined her choice of lovers.

And she reminds us that to find a good man, we need to find the good woman in us.

At the
D.C. Jail every Saturday, young black women line up for visits, many of them toting babies on their hips. Sometimes during peak hours, the line snakes outside the building.

I look at those women and think of many things. I think of the incarcerated men they love, and of the time when my daughter's father was in a military jail for going AWOL—when I dutifully caught a bus to another city to stand in line with our child on my hip. Above all, though, I think of myself, and the summer I went to jail. When I think about the trouble I got into, I worry even more about what will become of these young women. And I get the urge to tell them my story:

When I was in my late teens and early twenties, I was enamored of young black men who toted guns. These were guys who got their money through robberies or theft and usually spent some time in jail.

They thumbed their noses at the white establishment. I watched them from the window of my school bus, standing on the corner, smiling. I admired them; they were defiant enough to spend their days outside the classroom. "You get addicted to them," was how one fifteen-year-old mother put it to me recently, outside the D.C. Jail.

I saw them as daring and gutsy. Their behavior was an aphrodisiac. When you're a black child who believes she has no control over her life, you create your own definition of freedom.

These men exuded freedom. They controlled their lives, working when they wanted to and at what they chose to work at. At least that's the way it seemed in my small world, looking with my small eyes.

I also knew what kind of man I didn't want: a man like my father. He was a Marine, a flag-waving American. To me, he did everything The White Man said to do. He had been a part of the military that protected the racist society that I despised. I wore an Afro and refused to stand when I heard the national anthem, while he wore the same severe haircut he had worn as a soldier and took great pride in everything American. When blacks in Washington were rioting after the murder of Martin Luther King, my father turned to me and said, *"Your people are rioting."*

I thought I was a real revolutionary. I read Malcolm, H. Rap Brown, and George Jackson. But in reality, I was counterrevolutionary. The young men I dated were as detrimental to "the revolution" as the young black men who today kill other young black men over women or money or rocks of crack. Or for any reason.

Back then, I was living in the middle-class suburban Maryland town of Glenarden. If Theodore "The Beaver" Cleaver had been black, he would have lived around the corner. There were split-level homes with neat yards and flower beds. Yet when I looked at the neighborhood, I saw "sell-outs." To my young eyes, the only way a black family could get to the 'burbs was to sell its heart to the devil. To be removed from what I considered real life.

Deep inside, where my life's philosophy was fermenting, there was the belief that real life was something more nitty-gritty than the 'burbs. It was *adventure*—making up your own rules and knowing how to live "the street life."

My passport to such a life was men. What I didn't foresee was how much their lives would spill over into mine; how they would shape the choices I made. I was too young to know that in many ways you become who you love, but one day I would wake up and find that instead of simply sleeping with trouble, I was engulfed by it.

I listened to young men whisper about stolen cars and holdups and drugs. If you can't be powerful, I reasoned, you can at least be with those who are. After a while, though, it wasn't enough. I wanted the power I thought they possessed, and before long, I reached for it much as these young men did. For several years I held drugs, did drugs, and stole anything I wanted.

At first, our behavior seemed almost harmless. After all, I reasoned naively, who was getting hurt? These were guys who stole, sold "hot" merchandise, robbed people with guns they never used, or ran flimflam games. They didn't blow away people or make fortunes dealing drugs—as today's tough guys do. Respecting this code made them seem almost "good" to me.

Today's young women seem just as good at fooling themselves. Many of them love guys who are more than likely headed for jail. And though some I talked to said they wanted to get out of such relationships, most said they lacked the strength to change.

A generation has passed but the aphrodisiac hasn't lost its strength.

I saw my younger self in Darice. She was standing in the busy hallway of U.S. District Court early one morning not long ago, her hair immaculate and large. Darice, eighteen and a high school senior, was waiting for her brother's court appointment.

"I like guys who carry themselves like they're not weak" is the way she explained it. "I don't look for no car or care about the money." Her boyfriend, she said, is someone who makes a living "out in the street, but is respectful. He says he's in school, but he's not."

An unkempt twenty-two-year-old nodded her head in agreement. "I like guys who start fights, trying to protect their images. It's their masculinity. They have a sense of power," she said.

"Rude boys" is what Wilma, who lives in Southeast, calls them. One evening not long ago, Wilma, sixteen, was with her fourteen-year-old sister at the Parklands Community Center, where they drew pictures and cut out their designs.

Wilma wore big loop gold earrings and her hair in a ponytail. After she had ticked off the names of guys she's dated, she paused, then added, almost with surprise, "They've all been hustlers."

Francine, who wore gold earrings with her name spelled in them, conceded that money is beginning to mean more to her. She dates two boys. One "goes to church and everything. I think he sells [drugs] sometimes, when he needs money. The other one is out there twenty-four-seven," she said, meaning all the time.

Wilma, who said she wants "to be a secretary and work in Crystal City" when she grows up, said she and her sister are becoming more tempted to follow the example set by the boys they date. "Sometimes we think about selling drugs," she said.

At Superior Court, a plump sixteen-year-old sat waiting for her own case to be called. (She would not say why she was in court.)

"The boys I like are in school, but they don't go. They're out all hours, never stay in the house," she said. "My father was weak, so I was attracted to the boys who lead.

"I like that domineering type. I don't want someone who I can touch and they fall. I've been like this since I was thirteen. It's just a phase, I hope."

It was a fifteen-year-old mother of an infant, waiting to appear in court on truancy charges, who talked to me about being "addicted to them." She said she likes boys "who can fight to protect themselves. Sometimes I'm with them and I do what they do, and get in trouble."

My big trouble marked the beginning of the end of my love for tough guys. I was twenty-two, and the trouble came at a concert in Charlotte, N.C., when the man I was dating and a friend tried to sell marijuana to an undercover agent.

Before we left my apartment one of them asked me to put a packet in my purse. I knew it was heroin. When the police found the drugs on me, we were charged with possession of heroin with intent to distribute.

The detectives who questioned me demonstrated their power by getting the court to set my bond at $150,000. If I wanted out, I had to snitch on some big drug dealer. But the truth of the matter was I didn't know any dealers that fit their description of "big."

So I went to jail and spent the summer there, waiting for my trial. During that stretch of hot days, my definition of power and freedom changed. To be free was to be able to go outdoors and feel the heat of the sun, to go to my refrigerator, to touch my two-year-old daughter's face.

I spent my days and nights with about seven other women. We wore long green dresses, which we hemmed to miniskirt length with safety pins some of the women had hoarded. I slept on the top bunk of a steel bed with a thin, lumpy mattress. The only private place was a shower stall behind a curtain. There was no clock. Our meals were delivered on metal trays handed to us through a slot. Occasionally, a guard would allow us to march down to a room with vending machines, where we could buy candy or cookies. A real treat.

"You're gonna like the big jail," my cellmates told me, because they were sure I was going to serve time in the state institution. "In the big jail you get to wear some of your own clothes and you can go to school."

"I'm not gonna like the big jail at all," I kept saying.

My parents came down from Maryland to visit. I watched my mother's tears through the glass partition that prohibited me from wiping her cheeks. But it was another wrenching scene that pushed me to change.

Because my daughter wasn't allowed to visit me, my mother agreed to walk around to the side of the jail and hold her up. I peered out the narrow slit window; my father held her on his broad shoulders so I could get a good look. They pointed up toward my window.

I cried. I imagined them saying, "Look, your mother is up there." As I wept, a cellmate who had told me how much she missed her son patted my shoulders.

After that, I knew I would never go to the big jail.

My parents got me out on bond by putting up as collateral the house they owned—paid for, of course, by the jobs I hated, the money my father had earned in the Marine Corps and as a gravedigger at Arlington National Cemetery.

The lessons rolled my way. How ironic that my father, the man I did not admire, was the only man who could and would rescue me. And even more vivid was this: When I went to court, there were only three black people present: my mother, my father, and myself. Not one of us could decide what would happen to me next.

We were powerless. The guys I knew wielded power on the streets, not in the halls of justice or in the offices of politicians. Once I stepped off the streets, I was out of their world.

That thought slapped me into reality. "Once I'm outside this courtroom," I remember thinking for the first time, "only one person can decide what will happen to me: *Me.*"

My parents had tried to tell me, but my attention had been elsewhere. Still, I got a second chance. I didn't go to the big jail. I was put on probation for five years.

I often wonder where I would be if my parents had had to contend with a neighborhood filled with drugs, or with their ownpoverty and lack of education. I don't know if I would have made it.

I was lucky, and I know it. I was privileged too because, through it all, I knew there was an alternative to a life of crime. I knew I could own a house, because my parents had one. I knew I could have a career, and not just a job, because my father had had a career in the Marine Corps. I even knew I could go to college if I really wanted to go. It is much more difficult to convince a child who lives in a poor community, where the only people with money are drug dealers, that he or she can seize control of his or her life.

So I worry about the young girls who love the drug dealers and the hustlers, the little women I see in courtrooms at murder trials, holding babies on their laps. I worry about them and their children. When I look at them I don't just see who they are; I also see who they could become if they understood what real power is and where it lies.

My daughter is a college graduate, making a career in the public relations business. I decided twenty years ago to give her a chance by giving her a mother devoted to her well-being. But I had to spend a summer in jail to discover the truths that serve me now. To discover my own power, I had to commit crimes and be punished in uncountable ways. It was one helluva way to learn. But it was a way.

I look at those lines outside the jail and wonder: What price will my sisters have to pay?

"Marilyn"

from

The Habit of Surviving

KESHO
YVONNE SCOTT

When Kesho
Yvonne Scott signed my copy of her book The Habit of Surviving:
Black Women's Strategies for Life, *she wrote the inscription "Survival
ain't liberation."*

*The Black woman as mainstay and pillar is a powerful internalized
self-image. But how do you endow survival with grace and dignity? How
do you endure and not make endurance an end in itself?*

*Kesho Yvonne Scott's oral history of the lives of five woman whose
experiences span the forties to the present addresses these questions and
more. Scott, in the book, frames these compelling "herstories" in a frame-
work that is a vibrant dance of revelation. Each woman struggles with
issues unique to her historical moment as well as with dilemmas that are
passed down from generation to generation like a torch.*

*The excerpt that follows presents the story of Marilyn. Her voice is
street- and woman-wise, yet as fragile as the dreams she pursues from the
somnolent fifties to the turbulent sixties and seventies. Marilyn is at
various moments in this commentary a rebel, a fighter, lost, found, a
princess, a queen. But mostly through the desperate and the peace-of-
mind-times, she is a woman whose journey is continuous, because life
is too.*

Driving to Iowa City this time to see Marilyn made me very nervous. She was my aunt. I had known her all my life, but I was never going to know her like I was going to know her now. She had warned me, "You really want to know all that shit?" And now, recalling that challenge, I found myself perspiring. Her moving to Iowa and seeming to settle down did not change the fact that I had known her as a somewhat wild religious fanatic, and now she had put her religion down, changed her name, and was reading radical feminist literature. I had been the radical of the family, but as I entered Hawkeye Drive, headed for her apartment complex, walked through her door, and found myself looking at a forty-seven-year-old woman with an African wrap on her head, a flowing caftan, slippers, and a ring in her nose, backed up by silhouettes of African women's bodies on the wall, I knew she was not in Iowa just to get a degree, and she might now be more of an activist than I was. I knew I saw before me the real guerrilla that America had to reckon with.

She started telling me about what marriage was like in the fifties. This first revelation was followed by a litany of abortive quests for identity, betrayals by false social expectations, useless self-denials, and spurious successes. Through it all, writing sustained her, and in the end, writing saved her.

I had no idea that I was going to get married that day. It was not something I wanted to do. My father and his father got together, and because we were underage, took us down to the court. I remember going downtown in my school clothes. I was wearing white buck shoes and my school jacket. I was seventeen. The judge said, "Well, since you're here, we might as well marry you." So they got us married. Trapped. I felt trapped. September 24, 1956. There was no preparation for the marriage. I just got married, and I had no idea what was going to happen next.

> *Marriage in the fifties was considered the natural progression in the rites of passage from adolescence to adulthood. Sex within the confines of marriage guaranteed morality that would keep the girls "good." It was also a way to legitimize pregnancy. Young women were shunted off from or fled their parents' household to join another. Marilyn continued with the grim details of a fifties forced marriage, unplanned pregnancy, and attempted abortions.*

I went home after that, got my clothes and moved to my in-laws'—who I had just acquired that day. I must have seen them only three times in my life since I met Bobby in junior high school. I just moved in one hour. I guess I had to go because I don't ever remember being asked did I want to marry. I don't even remember any discussion except that I had run around a few weeks before trying to abort the baby. I mean, I did know how to do that. And not from my mother. Friends told me I could take some pills. I took some quinine to get rid of the baby until my head was ringing like a bell. It didn't work. I told my boy husband that I had taken quinine and he got furious. Wop! And wop again. He hit me and said, "Don't you ever try to kill my children." I mean he went crazy. And I was feeling trapped.

The women—my mother and his—were not directing things. And this was real confusing to me. Women had always been the one telling "mens" what to do. To suddenly have the men take over was real confusing. And here I was with a boy husband and my mother-in-law. She took us to our bedroom, offering me one of her housecoats and some bedroom shoes. And I thought to myself, This is the end. I couldn't go to college. I was gonna have a baby. And the women wasn't doing no talkin'. I know what they thought of "mens" and marriage. And it wasn't so much from a religious point of view, because they weren't religious. The women acted like life was just to be endured because you weren't gonna get no earthly reward. They also acted like "mens" was to be endured, too. I had had one hope. I could control my mind. I could go to college. This was the way out in 1956. And since I was pregnant now, there was no way out.

Sex was very different when it's in the back of a car than when it's in a strange house and with a boy husband who was unemployed in 1956. Sex was different when Eisenhower was president and Detroit niggers were neck-to-neck poor. Sex was something you was suppose to be smart enough to know without your mama ever having to tell you about. It was assumed that I was going to be smart enough to figure boys out. I don't remember Mama ever saying anything to me about boys being dangerous, but the attitude was that nobody took men seriously. I mean, that was the attitude. "Mens" was not to be taken as your friend. Not none of that Hollywood shit. Everybody knew that you would "fall in love" or you would have a man, but that was separate from what your other needs were. Your needs were met from women. I mean, men were expected to run around. They were expected to spend their money. They expected you to want their money. They was expected to be abusive. I had seen in the course of my growing up men beating women. Mr. Henry used to beat his wife outside so the neighbors would see her. I guess I thought that if you had a man you was gonna fight with him. You had a man just because, but you didn't take him on for any serious reasons. I knew about the menstrual cycle and getting pregnant, and when I started my period, at eleven, I can remember my family's response: Oh God, how inconvenient! Then I hid wearing a bra and everything from my mama.

Three weeks after I was married I remember going home and knocking on the door. My father answered. He looked at me and said to come on in. I was telling Mama how many problems I was having. Daddy interrupted and said, "You made your bed, so you gonna have to go back and lie in it." I had no other recourse. I couldn't come home. I was just like Daddy—who couldn't go home because he had made his bed in Baton Rouge, Louisiana, and he wasn't about to go home.

Marilyn's family reflects the common pattern of color, caste, and class-based marriage among blacks, especially in the fifties. An educated high-yellow mother and a "streetwise" darker father with a third-grade education amounted to a mixture of sex-role tensions between parents that, in turn, fostered sibling competition and struggles over beauty standards.

Daddy had been one of those people that when Henry Ford went to the South and said "five dollars a day," Daddy left. So he took Mr. Ford up on his word and hoboed on the train to Detroit. He had no education. I think about third or fourth grade at best. Daddy was a gambler and a storyteller. I can remember the time he told me the story about seeing his first automobile.

"I was walking home with my brother Oscar and seeing these tracks in the dust." Daddy started all of his stories with him and Oscar—"Oscar and me" or "Me and my baby brother, Oscar." Anyway, "We didn't know what these tracks was, so we thought they was snake tracks. So we hid in the bushes. Shortly we saw a thing coming down the road and it didn't have no horse pullin' it. We was absolutely petrified at the noise. So me and Oscar took a bush, because we thought the track was wicked and looked like snakes, and started scuffing the road until there was no more tracks. That way them snakes would never return."

As I said, Daddy was a storyteller. And his past was his reference point. And though I was fascinated listening to his stories, I just thought that he and Oscar were full of silliness. Daddy was always cutting language short, as Mama would say, because he couldn't pronounce certain words. He had been one of those "Creo niggers" from Louisiana, who were mixed with the French blood and ways.

I hear tell of Daddy having a lot of "street kids" (a bunch of babies by different women), but I was the only legitimate child he had. He had loved the trains as a boy, and he would tell these long stories about the magic of the railroad. When we left the housing projects, we moved to a dead-end street near the railroad track. The trains would go by and shake the house and that was a big thrill to him. Mama would get sick because she just thought it was horrible. Daddy thought it was just wonderful. So it was just from his two different connections, with the railroads and Louisiana, that I got a real sense of what was important about him. Knowing where and why trains were going was what Daddy thought was important. He just kept talking about the trains, telling his stories and using his dialect—he would not stand to be corrected by Mama. That's how I learned about Louisiana and Daddy and the South and music. He loved jazz. He loved the streets. He loved Mama. Himself and me.

Mama was an educated high-yellow black woman and was used to correcting everybody. She had graduated from high school and was a teacher. She went to Hampton University Normal School in Hampton, Virginia. It was equivalent to about the first year of college. Her folks was "North Carolina niggers." Ahoskie, North Carolina, niggers. And there is a strange tale here. I think the nickname for North Carolina people is "tarheels." Mama's people was heavily connected with Indian blood and ways. They were mixed peoples. Mixed peoples stayed mixed by marrying the "bluest-veined niggers" with the Indian features, to keep the color of the high yellow. They had dark hair and high cheek-bones. Straight long hair. They were the "pretty niggers." The "successful niggers." The niggers who got the education and the niggers who came to the North to tell the black blacks what to do and how to do it right.

She had come to Detroit during Depression years to get security. She had divorced her first husband, my brother's father, and was a follower of "Marcus Garvey's way of thinking": Be proud of the black man and use your skills for your race. Mama wanted a teaching job or a good job (anything other than domestic work). When she didn't see no good job for herself, she picked her a Northern man—Daddy—who was twelve years older than her and had a very secure factory job that put him in the black middle class. But there was a lot of disparity in our house. First, Daddy had no education and Mama did. His ego was always the problem. He felt that he was being put down a lot of times. Daddy liked to party, wear good clothes, and looked good in a suit. He'd come home from the foundry and bathe for two hours, dress up, and went out most nights. He wore the "Panama straw" of the neighborhood. It was the kind of hat Maurice Chevalier wore in the late thirties. Daddy also wore Edmond Clap shoes and silk stockings. Pomp and flash. Mama just accepted that his ways was what went with the territory of marrying this kind of man. Mama was not like this at all.

Second, there was disparity between how the family was split. I was my father's daughter and my brother was my mother's son. And there was a great difference in the way we looked. My brother looked like Mama's people and I had the yellow skin with Daddy's African-looking features. I had a sense of being ugly because of Mama's "North Carolina looks." Mama had felt like an ugly duckling herself because she was a lighter brown instead of a high yellow of almost white. It's like I could never get beyond the division. People kept telling me I looked just like my daddy. They didn't know it really hurt me because I wanted to look just like my mother. I wanted Mama to treat me just like she treated my brother. I thought that if I had only looked like my brother, things would be all right. Instead, I always had to answer these questions: "How come your brother is so fine?" "How come you don't look like him?"

And of course, my brother was also smart. He was five years older than I. He went to an all-white trade school. That was a really big deal because he was one of three blacks to get in. My mother was proud of her son. Daddy didn't pay no mind. I can remember that I used to always try to measure my grades against my brother's and I couldn't do it. There was always this business of his intelligence, and my father took offense to that.

I can remember my mother leaving my father at least on one occasion because he had been beating my brother. Daddy was very harsh to him. I was secretly happy about it. I felt like he got what he deserved because I couldn't get my mother's attention. And he could sing, too. He used to sing in the neighborhood church choir. However, my brother would bring into the house very different music. He liked "white music." Most black folks didn't listen to black entertainers like Billy Eckstine, who catered to white audiences. They listened to blues. I didn't listen to only black music. My brother and I liked Les Paul and Mary Ford.

Whenever anything electrical broke down in the house, my brother could fix it. He had a huge electrical plane and a crystal radio. He used to hang wires from the house to the trees in the front yard. We used to listen with headphones to the little crystal set. I can remember taking my friends upstairs to show them my brother's radio. I knew the other boys were jealous of him. He had a lot of problems being smart in the neighborhood. I admired him.

I was a tomboy and no one messed with me because I had an older brother. I hated dolls. I thought playing house was silly. I knew it wasn't what was expected of me. Mama expected me to use my head. I remember somebody gave me a black doll and I didn't want it. I wanted a white doll, and when I got it, I tore her blue eyes out for marbles. I wasn't interested in tea sets. I wanted to play with what my brother played with. He had an erector set and trucks, and I could tell that boys and girls were divided by the toys. I could see how they climbed trees and could pretend to be whatever they wanted. I understood what Mama meant when she said she "wanted to be born a man." I did too. It had something to do with seeing men have more freedom and everyone expecting them to go to college. It didn't mean getting married. For the girls, they was expected to keep their eyes on the right man and live through their husband's achievement. Mama had seen and done just that in Ahoskie. Her first husband had been a tobacco farmer, and the rest of her brothers worked as sharecroppers on a white family's pickle factory.

Better job opportunities was not the only thing "white folks let us have during the war," as my Daddy used to say. We lived in a newly built, government-sponsored housing project. It was designed for those "better Negroes" (meaning those who worked). We were happy to be there. We had a "real family," by white folks' standards. Daddy worked a steady job, Mama stayed home, and there were two kids. A older boy. A younger girl. By nigger standards, we was bourgeoisie. We was one of the few black families that had a new car—1936 Ford with a wheel on the back. It was a deluxe model. It was not raggedy. It was the kind of car rich white folks drove at the time. We was considered elite Negroes (acting like white folks) because Daddy had the car and Mama had the color.

I didn't have to think about white people. They were on the periphery of the ghetto. We talked about them in the context of them being storekeepers or as "the man pulling the strings." I knew they were people. I had white teachers, although I did not play with white children. My father and mother used to tell a lot of stories about white people. "They lynch niggers," my father used to say. Saying it another way, Mama talked about the NAACP and about some white man who painted his skin color black and went through the South pretending he was black. She said he later wrote a book about his experiences. She felt it was a great thing to do, exposing how Negroes couldn't drink from the white water fountains or use the white toilets. Daddy insisted that I ought to know, up front, that "the white people hate niggers." Mama quoted the papers about Emmett Till and I knew they was right.

There was a lot of privileges from "acting like white folks." Mama was always correcting me and my brother's language, so we had to speak a certain way. This meant the white teachers paid attention to me. They choose me over the other black girls. I was singled out by the teachers for the best books and games and rewards. And I wanted them. I worked ever harder. This kept me in trouble with my peers. I didn't always enjoy my "high-yellah" privileges.

Being elite, according to the neighbors, had a lot to do with skin color. I didn't view my color and sandy hair as no advantage. I had a lot of problems because the black-skinned girls said I thought I was "cute." I always had to figure out how to play in the games with other kids and not get beat up or not taking a bunch of shit from them.

I also went to the local public school. The other "yellow" kids went to Catholic schools. Mama and Daddy had the money but disliked that "religious stuff." Religion was something that we could pick and choose, and since the other kids were expected to go to church, I would go with them. Mama said, "It is the white man's bullshit to control the black man's mind." Daddy would go to church only so he could pick him a number and play it to make some money. He would play whatever the minister's verse was for that Sunday. His pet number was 213, and he made a lot of money gambling that number.

Gambling went along with living near Hastings Street. It was near downtown and near the biggest department stores. It was near the bus terminal (which would bring Negroes up from the South daily) and the Three Star Bar, where the pimps and prostitutes hung out. Me and my girlfriends used to sneak down by the bar to see the "nasty" women (prostitutes) and laugh and imitate them. They was mostly white. We also got to know who was the faggots. There were lots of gay men.

Hastings Street had the Entertainment Show Houses; the Eastern Fruit Market; the recording studio next to Sam's Music Shop (where we could watch the musicians making records); and the Brewster Center. This was where Joe Louis used to train when he was in town. He hadn't lived in the projects but this was where we could go and see his trophies. We used to listen to the Joe Louis fights on Hastings Street. Every store and home would have their radios on. When he would win, Hastings Street would be like Fifth Avenue in New York. Since we was poor people we used rolls and rolls of toilet paper for confetti and would run up and down the street. Joe Louis was a big, big deal. He was our only hero.

Mama used to talk about Mary McLeod Bethune and Walter

White of the NAACP because she was educated. The rest of the neighbors gossiped about black entertainers. Mama liked Pearl Bailey's and Lena Horne's singing and because they had married white men. She said "marrying white and staying black made them heroes to her."

I gained another hero in high school. Edgar Allan Poe. He was my star at Northeastern High School. Mama had insisted that we move out of the projects. By this time, my brother had married and Mama kept telling Daddy that the only way we could get ahead of "white folks" was to get some property. She wanted a house. Daddy was fifty-nine and wanted to stay with his "street buddies." During the war, he had made enough money at Ford's to buy a house, but Mama believed he had nothing to show because we still lived in the projects. So we moved into a house.

The neighborhood and new Northwestern High School had a bunch of middle-class niggers. They made me uncomfortable. I thought they talked funny. They talked like "white folks." We called them sissy. So I maneuvered to go to the Northeastern High School near the projects with my friends. I got into a trade curriculum to study tailoring. The mornings were tailoring classes and the afternoon I took electives. I was assigned a literature course that had a white gay teacher. There were several gay teachers but it wasn't a big thing then that gay people couldn't teach your children. We were grateful to have any teacher that would teach black folks. We had two black and one white gay teachers.

Mr. Riapell was white and gay and my literature teacher. He read Poe one day in class and my head spun around. I guess I heard romantic sounds. That's when I decided to be a poet. I was in the eleventh grade. Things began to clear up when I decided myself I was going to be a poet. I remember telling Mama. She didn't think it was odd. I think she connected it with teaching poetry. She didn't laugh. She knew I was a thinker. After that, high school became interesting. I dropped tailoring and took up college preparatory courses. I was in the top 5 percent of my class. I got heavy duty into literature courses and public speaking. I was vice president of my senior class. I can remember my father asking my mother when did he have to get the money for me to go to college. I got excited. I loved school. I was expected to go to Wayne State University, which was right on the other side of the projects. I wasn't expected to get pregnant. I got pregnant. Daddy was devastated. Disappointed, Mama shook her head and said, "I thought you knew better. I thought you knew to use something." I wish I knew to use something, too.

I sat on the bed with my boy husband, frightened. He was trapped. I was trapped. Thinkin' aloud: This is my end.

Although the role models for blacks in the fifties were sparse, one of the more common was the assertive women who did day work. Marilyn found herself in awe of and intimidated by the women in her husband's household who held such jobs.

Living with my in-laws, I learned about the "fuck you women." Bobby's mother was a "fuck you woman." She had three of her sisters in the house with her. They was the kind of women who told a man, "Fuck you and get up and get it yourself." I had never seen these kind of women. You were expected to strategize around a man or make him think it was his idea—if you had one—but telling a man "fuck you, do it yourself" was unbelievable.

I remember Mama arguing with Daddy until he turned to fighting. Then she'd give up. But not Bobby's mother. She had the best way of saying "shit" that's ever been said in the world. No one to this day can say "shit" like she can. It was like poetry. She would say "fuck you" and "shit" to her husband and then she'd break up everything in the kitchen. I thought this was marvelous. I can remember she wanted a kitchen sink that cost eight hundred dollars. That was unheard of in the fifties. Her husband said no. She'd say "fuck you," and the next thing I knew, Sears was out putting in a new sink. I listened to these women from our small bedroom on the third floor. I would cheer them on. Right on! They were the first women I saw who worked consistently.

Mama had worked a stretch during and after the war. More for herself than for having to provide extra money for the household. Some of her happiest days were when she was working in the factory with women. She used to come home and talk about the women and how they formed a really close community. Even the white women. I had viewed white women as inferior. I thought they were "silly women," from the stories I had heard about them. Mama said the camaraderie of the women in the factory was strong because they all were glad to go to work. I can remember it was a real accomplishment to have a working mother who didn't work in white folks' houses. Bobby's mother was a cook and her sisters did day work. They worked for white folks and they came in from a full day's work and said "fuck you" whenever it suited them.

I was scared to be a "fuck you" woman. I was scared of everything. I was scared when the doctor gave me a pelvic exam. I was scared when my boy husband kept referring to the baby as his child and how happy he was that he was married. I was scared when I didn't feel like reading Edgar Allan Poe. I got scared when I was asked to cook on the second day of marriage. I knew nothing about cooking and cleaning. I knew nothing about having a baby or being a wife. I knew about literature.

> *Motherhood was a mixed blessing for Marilyn. A premature baby reinforced her sense of inadequacy and entrapment. A move away from her in-laws, as an army wife, began to reshape her identity. Typically, however, traditional sex roles in her marriage replaced earlier parental domination and led to a different and equally disempowering sense of frustration.*

The baby was born early. He weighed three pounds and seven ounces. He had to be put in an incubator. The doctors didn't know if he was going to live or die. I was concerned about him living, from a human point of view. But I knew I wouldn't be terribly distraught if he had died. I didn't like the whole setup. I wanted out of the marriage. I thought if he died, my father would let me come back home. I didn't have to stay married. I could go to college. My son came home from the hospital and tightened the trap. I resigned myself to this thought: This was the way my life was going to be.

My boy husband and I decided he would go into the army to get a job. They were accepting families with one child. His mother didn't like the idea. Although I enjoyed the women in the house, watching all the freedom they had to come and go, I wanted something for myself. My boy husband and the women in the house thought of me as Bobby's wife. I was not real to them. I didn't have an identity. I was the babymaker and the one that kept their lineage. So I wanted out. The thought of going somewhere, anywhere, was wonderful to me. He went to Fort McMacklin for basic training. There was no room for privates' wives on the base, so we took a small apartment miles away. Bobby came home on weekends. I was a wife only on weekends. I had my own space. I had not counted on the isolation.

I had absolutely nothing to do during the week. I was not a group person. Once I got pregnant in high school, I didn't have girlfriends because their mothers didn't want them to associate with me. When I was a married woman I lost all my male friends. So I had to deal with spending a lot of time by myself. Alone. I decided after a month to move back home with my parents. This time I could come home because I was married and I had a child. I finally achieved some status. I was married and a mother and a black who had traveled. I had ridden a plane. It was not travel to come from the South to the North. I had traveled as an army wife. I got army wife's pay. My father was delighted.

Bobby was shipped out to Santa Fe, New Mexico. This was perfect. We were away from his family and mine. I fell in love with the Southwest. I had two more babies in New Mexico. The first, another son, died deformed. So here I was in a married army barrack with two kids. Bobby busy in the army in a peacetime war, and I stuck like a bunch of women left at home. I didn't mix with the women. All they talked about was baby diapers. I turned to reading. I would go to the library. I read all day. The fact that I had gotten away from Detroit and was living differently than the folks at home didn't feel so much like a trap.

I loved this setup in New Mexico. Bobby didn't. He wanted to come home. We did. And it seemed like there I was in a cell again. We moved back with the in-laws and then to a public housing project. Bobby wanted a wife that cooked, a wife that smiled when she took care of the children, and a wife that listened to everything he was doing and where he was going in his world. I was restless. I wanted to work. I saw myself doing something in the way of a career. He saw me in connection to what he was doing. I had nothing to call my own. The children belonged to him. Being his wife, I belonged to him. His career belonged to him. I wanted something that was mine. I just didn't know what it was.

The watershed of change garnered from the Civil Rights movement created a host of opportunities for education and career development for blacks. Marilyn's quest to study literature, which could have been furthered by these changes, only precipitated problems at home and at school. Confronted with racial prejudice in the classroom when she did try to escape and constrained by a husband made jealous by her attempts to get an education, she lapsed again into self-abnegation.

"The white folks are paying for us to go to college." That's what my girlfriend had said, and I was off to get the money to go. I got a National Defense Student Loan. You had to pay it back, but I didn't even think of that. There was an avenue out, I thought.

I had to sell Bobby on the idea. I strategized so he would let me go to school as long as I supported him at what he was doing. We moved into the Jefferies Project, which had student housing just three blocks from Wayne State University. Daddy had just retired from the factory in 1962, so he could pick up the kids Monday,

Wednesday, and Friday, while I went to school. And Bobby would pick them up at night. I hadn't prepared to be thrown into a classroom with middle-class blacks. I also didn't take into account Bobby's insecurities would come out.

I was intimidated by their age. There was a vast difference in experience. I spoke in an East Side slang. These middle-class niggers were embarrassed by me every time I raised my hand to ask a question. I also did not know how to study. It finally dawned on me that I couldn't write a simple sentence. I was failing. I had not even thought of any of these possibilities. My instructor called me into his office and asked me what my major was. I said "English." He choked and calmly said, "I can't pass you. Your papers are absolutely terrible." I was devastated. Here I was again, another failure. I can remember him taking a book off the shelf, throwing it in my lap and saying, "Go home and teach yourself how to write and speak English. I'll take you next semester. And I'll let you write what you want to write. You don't have to follow the class subject but you have to write if you say you want to be a writer."

I was angry and humiliated. I had the summer off, read the book, and wrote my first paper. A long poem. It was called "The Bulldozer." It was about white people coming down in the black community and bulldozing our neighborhoods. This is what they called urban renewal. I used to watch the bulldozers and think, You're sweeping away the houses and you're sweeping away the weeds, but where are you sweeping the people? My teacher was shocked. I was still saying I wanted to be a poet, so he took me to the then poet laureate of the college and asked him to read my work. The poet asked if I was the one who had failed his colleague's class. I nodded. He told my instructor, "She writes very well." He called it intuitive writing. I laughed because I didn't know all that structure and theory. When we read Homer of the *Iliad* or *Odyssey* and shit, it didn't mean anything to me. The instructor let me write what I wanted to write after that and I did. I wrote about what I knew about and that was my life. I wrote about growing up and being black. After this, school was very, very, very interesting.

Bobby reacted. He saw school as a threat to him somehow. He expected me to do everything in the house, study when he wasn't home, and, worst, accused me of having a "nigger on the side." I could never stay at school to study after that. I could never study at home, with the arguments and kids. My grades started to slip, the fighting started, and all that talk about being a poet and writer and maybe someday teaching and having a career seemed like such a distance away. I stopped the fighting because I took everything in the house and broke it like his mother. He quit beating me. But I was already beat. So the long and short of it was I quit school. Trapped again.

Faced with failure in school and the locked door of domestic life, Marilyn joined an organized religion. For a time she found a purpose for her talents and an avenue for self-expression. Even religion offered less solace when she discovered that it, too, supported her entrapment. Her new-found freedom was, again, challenged by her husband. The consequences this time were divorce, single parenthood, returning home to elderly parents, and a search for employment, although she had no marketable skills or experience.

Being depressed and seeing Bobby's career moving forward and the kids growing, I turned to God. I started studying the Bible. I had the help of other members of a door-to-door ministry. They were coming by and teaching me. At first, I wasn't interested in religion but I did like their approach to the Scriptures and the business of the teaching process. Learning began to take a lot of time and filled my emptiness. I began to enjoy the Scriptures and I was becoming disillusioned about school. I began to think of school and all this talk about being a poet as fairyland. And not knowing what to do, I got pregnant. I could get Bobby off my back about going to school, I could study the Scriptures at home, and I could tell myself I was a realist.

Sometimes, I could get out of the house and attend church meetings, participate in door-to-door ministry, and talk to new people about something that was important to me. My religion had an international perspective. I expected to minister someday in Africa, and I met members from all over the world. I felt like I was involved in an international organization. It was grander than the storefront churches in the ghetto. And I felt that my church was calling black women to play an important role in the ministry. I felt we had a real heavy-duty part to play in international affairs. So the religious organization kept me traveling and I was satisfied. My third son was born, Bobby was hired by a large manufacturing company, and I was traveling a bit—and this seemed like a way out. I was satisfied. Bobby got a career and I'm doing religion. And I'm getting damned good at it. I'm teaching and I'm enjoying it. I got a vision. I've got something that belongs to me, and Bobby is tearing up my religious books now.

"Give it up or I'll leave." Bobby put it to me plain. Give it up or lose the house, security, and good sex. Be my wife and nothing else. By this time, he's become a fighter again on a regular basis. And generally the fights would come before the fuck. I was very definite as to when I wanted it and when I didn't. So we fought. Verbally and physically. He'd say I was a bitch and a whore. I was getting tired of fighting and being attacked about my religion and perplexed about trying to live up to the Bible Scriptures: Whatever the man does, a woman should accept that. You're supposed to take it. Even when he is physically beating your ass. And I don't like the fact that I'm feeling foolish. I mean that doesn't make sense to me. The *t* in "trapped" is filling up again. And this time, I've got three kids and a man I can't live with no more and no education and a no-making-sense religion that I enjoy that says "take it"—and I still don't have nothing that's really mine.

I choose God. Bobby leaves and tells me I'll have to crawl back. I go home to Daddy again. I got no job. I was absolutely scared to go out and get a real job. I went down to the unemployment office in the city of Detroit. They kept asking me if I could type. I couldn't type. Then they gave me nineteen million forms to fill out and I was exhausted. I got to this desk and the receptionist asked me a simple question and I blew up. I started screaming about not having a job and having three babies to feed. I was hysterical. A tall black woman came up to me and asked me to sit down and calm down. I was mumbling underneath my breath that "this was a bunch of shit, these people ain't gonna get me no job." "I'll have a job for you in two days," she said. And she did. This was just a few months after the Detroit riot of 1967.

I had applied to the phone company three times. Before the riots, they weren't hiring Negroes, now called blacks. I got the job as one of the direct benefits of the riot. I was making $78.50 a week. I was a technician. I put in the cable so homes could get personal dial tones. They needed women to handle the equipment because of the dexterity of our hands. At first, we was hired together. Black and white women. The white women got promoted for management. We were kept on the lower echelons but we didn't complain because this was the best salary some of us had ever had. So all the black women did the physical work, up and down those cable ladders, and the white women became supervisors. Every once in a while, a hillbilly would stay amongst us. She was generally considered a "white trash" type of white anyway. The union didn't look out for her or me.

It was a small office and I was scared of being fired at any time. At least for the first year. The thought of not being able to feed my children was terrifying. I was never late or absent. In fact, I remember calling my kids and making it clear that they were not to call me on the job unless it was a real emergency. They had to take care of themselves. After a while the job got routine. I also knew the bosses didn't know from one minute to the next what the fuck we were doing. We weren't supervised. So I made a big production about everything I was doing to appear busy. To appear like a good worker. That way I didn't have to work that hard. I could bullshit them the way they bullshitted me come evaluation time. The way I saw it, as women, we were both fucking animals trying to cover our asses.

Seven or eight years later, they made me management and sent me to a branch office. It was an all-black office with a white supervisor. I had the job of managing black people. I was a "straw boss," as my Daddy used to say. That's a boss with no power. A boss can be a function or a head. I could make no decisions. I couldn't hire or fire anybody. I couldn't set up any plans of how I wanted the job to go without checking with my boss. And I especially didn't like the fact that my supervisor could tell me how to treat black people. So I quit and went back to the cable lines with the rest of the black women. I didn't see it as a career. In fact, black women that I know didn't use that word. I felt I was part of production. I learned the job and I was supposed to do it. Not thinking about it. If someone had asked me what I wanted to do for my life, it certainly would not be working for the phone company.

I got an apartment a few doors from my aging parents. I got my own money and it seems OK. I'm active with my church and I have a way to support my kids and myself. Bobby is darting back and forth through the door saying "the marriage can resume any time you're ready to quit that religion," and I've got my eye on putting some money together and traveling. Thinking about Daddy and how he watched those trains.

Although she was meeting the challenge of being on her own, Marilyn became disillusioned with her life when the racism in her church became clear to her. Living alone and sexless, she embarked on still another quest—a disastrous search for a mate, which led to her attempted suicide.

Mexico was a good way to make a start after the divorce. I enjoyed it. Although I'm living a very tight life in terms of men because of my religion, I'm on the move. I'm taking trips now all the time. I'm enjoying ministering. Mama points out to me that I'm not saving money to do anything. She thinks I should spend more time with the kids. It was a repeat of what she had told Daddy: "Get some property and buy a house."

I reacted like an animal in a cage because I don't want no house.

I'm paying sixty dollars a month and living in a condemned building but it's giving me the money to travel. Traveling is what is most important to me, not buying a house. I'm doing well at the telephone company and they keep giving me promotions. Bingo! More money to travel. I'm doing well in my church and traveling all over the world now, speaking about the "Truth." Things appear to be going well. And by now I'm beginning to see the racism in the church. I see the great disparity between how black poor people live under the tenets of religion and how white people live their lives. I see how black converts living in the inner city took shit jobs to devote more of their lives to religious work, and whites had professional jobs and took vacations. I reacted to the church views looking down on education because I wanted to translate my spiritual vision into writing. I need to translate the Bible into me and Daddy's language, and I need to move this organization, like Mama said, "to save black people."

I began to see more clearly the power of "male rule," which puts women, who do all the work, in the very lowest level in the organization. And I admit to myself that I am in a religious organization that is sexist and segregated and I have been in it for twenty years. Then the trap begins to close in on me. In the back of my head, I'm thinking about the confines of the religion in terms of relationships. It's demanding marriage as a way of exercising sex. But I know the prospect of somebody marrying me with three kids and a strong religion is slim. So I'm feeling the pressure of being alone. I want my husband back (who by now is living with this woman). And I know I don't want to marry a man in my church. They seem like sissies to me. And the "street niggers" won't accept my church. I need a man and sex, and the religion makes me feel useless without a man. I'm feeling odd and confused because I know a sense of self doesn't come from a man. I'm getting tired again. Mama and Daddy are getting older. Mama won't go out of the house and Daddy's behavior is getting crazier and crazier. And the trap is tightening again. The only way out . . . is traveling, and I'm doing it every goddamn chance I can get. But to travel, that means I've got to work ten hours a day. And I'm tired. So I take a chance to get out.

I started going with a fellow from high school. He says "marriage" and I feel it will give me validity in the community. I'm viewing this man as a way out. He won't join my church, but he will be my husband. I'm needing to get some rest somewhere. I feel real tired. I'm exhausted. So on my way to work one morning, about six o'clock, I decided to stop at his house because he was on my mind and a woman answers the door. I was shocked. She says, "Who in the fuck are you?" I ask her, "Who in the fuck are you?" "I'm his wife!" And I swallow twenty-seven sleeping pills. I go out. I really want out. So I lay down in the middle of the street.

I end up in a psycho ward. I'm spitting up my shit. I'm groggy. I'm coming in and out of reality. I am in rage. Everybody asking me why I did it. I keep saying "fuck you" and they call Mama. But Daddy comes down to the hospital and I tell him to go get fucked. Finally, the doctor says if I don't cooperate, then they are going to chain me to the bed. I stop cussing and ranting. I get real quiet. "If you don't tell us why you did this, we're going to send you to Eloise" [the state mental hospital]. And I know he means it. And I'm trapped. So I say, "I really don't give a fuck what you do to me, but if I get out of here I'll never have reason to return again. I will never suffer this kind of defeat again."

The doctor is intensely listening to me now and taking me real seriously. "I know you saved my life and I'm not that insensitive to not say thank you. But I'm not going to be in here again." He believes me and releases me. "I wish you would consider outpatient therapy," he says. "I don't have no time to go to therapy. I gotta work. I have older parents and children and I have this and that . . . to do." And I'm thinking now, Twenty years in the religion and it has failed me. My friends pick me up and were silent all the way home.

Mama says, "I hope your brother doesn't find out," and I turn and say, "Don't worry, they not gonna put this in the paper." So I decide I have to decide something. I decide, Marilyn, you tried every way that you know how to set your mind free and don't look like you're doing such a good job, so the best thing you can do from heretofore is to try to make the best of a real bad situation. And that's what I did.

The death of her parents, an "empty nest," and an unfulfilling though secure job opened Marilyn up to a lesbian affair. More restless searching eventually led her back to school, and most importantly, to writing.

Daddy died first and Mama two years later. I went to Spain, and the kids were leaving, one by one. One marries and the others go to college. I'm making all kinds of money at the telephone company. I do buy the house and it's all working. Somewhere I'm getting back on the track. I take a woman lover. I didn't think of it as a lesbian experience. I think of it as something to fill the "dying inside" part of me. And Gina becomes part of my life. For the first time there is somebody that was anticipating my moods and what I want first and not making a judgment on it. She spends her time nurturing me. Picking over me. She picks my movies. My clothes. My hairstyles. She becomes my therapist and she puts me back together again. Humpty Dumpty style. Piece by piece. But the pieces aren't quite fitting, but she is trying. Slowly I'm coming together. I don't know what Gina is getting from this, but she is making the difference between whether I want to breathe one minute or the next. And she is wanting exclusive devotion. I feel trapped. Somehow, I'm feeling my space is being taken away again. So I ended it. Remembering the twenty-seven pills, I decided I was going to see my life through. I was going to put my head on in one direction. Period. So I missed the men in many, many ways, but the exchange was suffocation and I couldn't do either. So I started running.

I started this Toronto thing. Every six weeks. It was a place where I could feel pretty good about myself. No one knew me and no one cared. I'm thinking life is a big joke anyway. The nest at home is cleared out and in some sense I'm scared because soon there will be nobody to buy shoes for and no coats to get and everybody doing their own thing. That gives me all the time to run the streets. I'm running as far and wide as I can because I don't know: What is my thing?

College. Poetry. Writing. Came up again. So I decide to take a class. Not for a degree. I take two classes—poetry and literature. The poetry class is filled and requires that you have five poems written for entrance. By this time I have completely missed the sixties. Bits and pieces of it filtered into my life but I felt sorry that I missed a many-splendored thing.

And there are black poets now with loud revolutionary voices. There are black women's poetic voices, too! Poetry to me was like singing the blues. It was about: the man leaving, the bills unpaid, the pain of being black in America and the shit that gets dumped on you 'cause you got a pussy. So I go home and write five poems. The instructor reads them and lets me in. She ask the first day, "Who is Marilyn?" I raise my hand and it starts. She would put a word on the board and tell me to get up and show the class how to write a poem. I wrote and wrote. She kept after me and now I know I'm a poet. I'm a real poet because I'm doing it. I start saving my work and I start reading it over the radio and at poetry workshops and in bars. And I'm feeling. Just feeling. Me.

Accidently, I take a class taught by Mary Helen Washington and lo and behold I learn that black women are writing books. And that's the first time I hear about Margaret Walker, Alice Walker, Toni Cade Bambara, Toni Morrison, Gloria Naylor, Zora Neale Hurston—and I see women telling stories, using my Daddy's language and from our point of view. I can't afford her class, so she lets me monitor it. I hear black women's voices and I decide that I want to be one of those black women. Writing.

Really writing. So I start a novel in between the phone company and the ritual of church and trips to Toronto.

The novel was taking up my time, but the emptiness returned for the man. So I put it down. I remarried a younger man. An African who really wanted a green card. And I really wanted to play "African Queen." He was exotic and macho. We both got what we wanted and divorced. I decided to take a trip to Kenya. They welcomed me. Going to Africa was like making a connection to my mother and father. It was real important to me to talk to the women and make that international connection with them. I was surrounded by black people running everything and it felt good. I felt good.

By now I'm pushing eighteen years with the telephone company. The grandkids are born and I ain't no grandma type. I got a house I don't need, and a cushion of money, so I move into a luxury apartment in the suburbs. Southfield. That's where the "middle-class niggers" go, and I guess I'm middle class now. I've got a car. I've got all the things that would seem that people wanted. Although, I'm feeling religiously bankrupt. I don't feel comfortable calling on the "Father" anymore. And by this time I'm reading about women's spirituality and I'm real confused. I feel displaced. I'm in a lot of pain. And it's a trap. So I start to write again.

"Why don't you come to Iowa?" my niece said. I didn't know where the fuck Iowa was! I had no idea it was on the other side of Chicago. I thought it was in the Southwest and I loved the Southwest. So I go to Iowa. I thought: Why the fuck not!

The long and short of it is, I apply to the University of Iowa and they want me. I can get that minority money and cheap housing. And all I know is that I don't know how I gonna go to school and work. What kinds of jobs are there in Iowa? Yet, I'm tired of working. And I want to go to school. But I don't want to leave the phone company—my pension—and have nothing. I'm confused. Scared. I don't see how these pieces of me are all gonna come together. I think my niece was full of bullshit because she ain't old and she got two degrees and she's talkin' about me leaving everything. So I go home.

My niece sends me a story she writes for a class. I am the writer in the family and she wants my approval. I am jealous. She doesn't define herself as a writer. She defines herself as a sixties radical. I sure ain't that. But I am a writer and she's doing the writing. And she keeps asking me "what do you want to do" and I say "write" and she says "come to Iowa" and I say "I ain't got no money" and she says "yes you do, you can get financial aid." That shocks the shit out of me. It means I can come to school and I don't have to work.

I recognize this ain't got nothing to do with money. I see myself as a spiritual person and I ain't got faith in me from twenty years in religion. And my niece, who was my brother's child, was showing a lot of faith in me, and she didn't even know me. So I know. I never really tested myself against myself. I never really had a chance to take a challenge without the babies' wants and the "mens'" wants and the parents' wants and the bill collectors' wants. Just for me. I freak out when a poem of mine wins second place in a State of Iowa poetry contest. And I'm dreaming, every night in Detroit, of coming to school in the summer. The mailman brings a letter saying I got the money. I mean I'm really shocked. I go to work and give them my two weeks' notice, pack up my shit in a U-Haul, and a week later, I'm on the road to Iowa. And as I'm driving here, I'm remembering what my boss said: "We can only give you thirty days off and after that you don't have a job." And I'm thinking, Well, you're gonna take another shot at this college shit at forty-six? And what makes you think you can do something at forty-six that you couldn't do at twenty-six?"

I'm in Iowa. Classes begin in three days. I'm feeling like I ain't got no money. I need a job. My niece arranges an interview for me for the position of librarian at the Women's Resource and Action Center, and I get it. So I've got a job. I've got my own space. I've got my books and I'm working with women. And it's all happening at once. I mean all of it, it's coming together. I'm scared because school might really work. I'm scared because I am writing my ministry. And, I'm really, really scared that I might really be me.

> Marilyn's interpretation of her life exposes the complex dynamics of how she was oppressed within her family and society. Her story tells where, how, and why, through private rebellions, she simultaneously resisted and adapted to that oppression as a kind of "loyal opposition." Marilyn believed other women seemed to have fewer options than she did. So when she looked out in the world and realized what she could change was limited, she rationalized. If she could not change her family, community, or the world, she could change what was in her head. Acting out an internal theater of "antagonistic cooperation," she apparently went along with what she did not like.

> Her story is very complicated, and lives like hers have always been close to invisible. They have been invisible to American history, white feminism, and Afro-American male-centered history. It is only with the success of black women writers, whose work "spoke" to Marilyn as it has to so many others, that such stories have begun to surface.

> Marilyn had the habit of surviving through private rebellions. The failure of such private rebellions is that they develop skills that at one level seem admirable, indeed are admirable—such as cunning, patience, and the ability to rationalize unpleasant realities—but never lead to complete liberation. One adapts from within.

> Marilyn adapted to the existence of an intraracial color-caste system; she adapted to a forced marriage of the fifties; she adapted to the roles of mother and wife. And the price she paid for these habits of surviving was denial of large parts of herself. She had internalized the many external features of oppression. She denied that she was a writer; she denied that she was a leader; she denied that she wanted to be part of a worldwide revolutionary ministry.

> Private rebellions—in this case masked as suppressions—never challenged the institutional features of her oppression in family or in society. More open rebellions and efforts at self-liberation would have moved her beyond a habit of survival and its corresponding adaptive skills. They would have required disengagement from not only conventional female

roles but from those roles sculpted by black family life and by white society which made any kind of black family life even more difficult. Not surprisingly, this was not possible for Marilyn until later in her life —and until the times were comparatively more open. The eighties, after all, were not the fifties.

Divorce, grown children, and a job with seniority—it wasn't until Marilyn had all these things that she could consider liberation. By forty-six, she was prepared to take these risks. She knew by then that survival was a lot, but that it was not enough.

Uses of the Erotic:

The Erotic as Power

AUDRE LORDE

Audre Lorde *was the consummate Woman Warrior. A poet of eloquence and passion, she lived her life as though IT was the revolution. She was a lesbian who never let that designation separate her from women who were not, or from a community that swore, Not my daughter, Not my son, in response to the reality that gay men and women are our sons and daughters, our mothers and fathers.*

Audre Lorde's life was a relentless exploration and rejection of the political and sexual canon that binds our minds as tightly as Chinese women's feet once were. The following essay is a sexual manifesto exploring the power source most frequently denied by society and ignored by women—the erotic. Just as her poems subvert the expected, here Lorde broadens the meaning and possibility of our use of the word, our belief about what it means and is.

There are many kinds of power, used and unused, acknowledged or otherwise. The erotic is a resource within each of us that lies in a deeply female and spiritual plane, firmly rooted in the power of our unexpressed or unrecognized feeling. In order to perpetuate itself, every oppression must corrupt or distort those various sources of power within the culture of the oppressed that can provide energy for change. For women, this has meant a suppression of the erotic as a considered source of power and information within our lives.

We have been taught to suspect this resource, vilified, abused, and devalued within Western society. On one hand, the superficially erotic has been encouraged as a sign of female inferiority—on the other hand, women have been made to suffer and to feel both contemptible and suspect by virtue of its existence.

It is a short step from there to the false belief that only by the suppression of the erotic within our lives and consciousness can women be truly strong. But that strength is illusory, for it is fashioned within the context of male models of power.

As women, we have come to distrust that power which rises from our deepest and nonrational knowledge. We have been warned against it all our lives by the male world, which values this depth of feeling enough to keep women around in order to exercise it in the service of men, but which fears this same depth too much to examine the possibilities of it within themselves. So women are maintained at a distant/inferior position to be psychically milked, much the same way ants maintain colonies of aphids to provide a life-giving substance for their masters.

But the erotic offers a well of replenishing and provocative force to the woman who does not fear its revelation, nor succumb to the belief that sensation is enough.

The erotic has often been misnamed by men and used against women. It has been made into the confused, the trivial, the psychotic, the plasticized sensation. For this reason, we have often turned away from the exploration and consideration of the erotic as a source of power and information, confusing it with its opposite, the pornographic. But pornography is a direct denial of the power of the erotic, for it represents the suppression of true feeling. Pornography emphasizes sensation without feeling.

The erotic is a measure between the beginnings of our sense of self, and the chaos of our strongest feelings. It is an internal sense of satisfaction to which, once we have experienced it, we know we can aspire. For once having experienced the fullness of this depth of feeling and recognizing its power, in honor and self-respect we can require no less of ourselves.

It is never easy to demand the most from ourselves, and from our lives, and from our work. To go beyond the encouraged mediocrity of our society is to encourage excellence. But giving in to the fear of feeling and working to capacity is a luxury only the unintentional can afford, and the unintentional are those who do not wish to guide their own destinies.

This internal requirement toward excellence which we learn from the erotic must not be misconstrued as demanding the impossible from ourselves or from others. Such a demand incapacitates everyone in the process, for the erotic is not a question only of what we do. It is a question of how acutely and fully we can feel in the doing. For once we know the extent to which we are capable of feeling that sense of satisfaction and fullness and completion, we can then observe which of our various life endeavors bring us closest to that fullness.

The aim of each thing which we do is to make our lives and the lives of our children more possible and more rich. Within the celebration of the erotic in all our endeavors, my work becomes a conscious decision—a longed-for bed which I enter gratefully and from which I rise up empowered.

Of course, women so empowered are dangerous. So we are taught to separate the erotic demand from most vital areas of our lives other than sex. And the lack of concern for the erotic root and satisfactions of our work is felt in our disaffection from so much of what we do. For instance, how often do we truly love our work?

The principal horror of any system which defines the good in terms of profit rather than in terms of human need, or which defines human need to the exclusion of the psychic and emotional components of that need—the principal horror of such a system is that it robs our work of its erotic value, its erotic power and life appeal and fulfillment. Such a system reduces work to a travesty of necessities, a duty by which we earn bread or oblivion for ourselves and those we love. But this is tantamount to blinding a painter and then telling her to improve her work, and to enjoy the act of painting. It is not only next to impossible, it is also profoundly cruel.

As women, we need to examine the ways in which our world can be truly different. I am speaking here of the necessity for reassessing the very quality of all the aspects of our lives and of our work.

The very word "erotic" comes from the Greek word *eros,* the personfication of love in all its aspects—born of Chaos, and personifying creative power and harmony. When I speak of the erotic, then, I speak of it as an assertion of the life-force of women; of that creative energy empowered, the knowledge and use of which we are now reclaiming in our language, our history, our dancing, our loving, our work, our lives.

There are frequent attempts to equate pornography and eroticism, two diametrically opposed uses of the sexual. Because of these attempts, it has become fashionable to separate the spiritual (psychic and emotional) away from the political, to see them as contradictory or antithetical. "What do you mean, a poetic revolutionary, a meditating gunrunner?" In the same way, we have attempted to separate the spiritual and the erotic, reducing the spiritual thereby to a world of flattened affect—a world of the ascetic who aspires to feel nothing. But nothing is further from the truth. For the ascetic position is one of the highest fear, the gravest immobility. The severe abstinence of the ascetic becomes the ruling obsession. And it is one, not of self-discipline, but of self-abnegation.

The dichotomy between the spiritual and the political is also false, resulting from an incomplete attention to our erotic knowledge. For the bridge which connects them is formed by the erotic —the sensual—those physical, emotional, and psychic expressions of what is deepest and strongest and richest within each of us, being shared: the passions of love, in its deepest meanings.

The considered phrase "It feels right to me" acknowledges the strength of the erotic into a true knowledge, for what that means and feels is the first and most powerful guiding light toward any understanding. And understanding is a handmaiden which can only wait upon, or clarify, that knowledge, deeply born. The erotic is the nurturer or nursemaid of all our deepest knowledge.

The erotic functions for me in several ways, and the first is in the power which comes from sharing deeply any pursuit with another person. The sharing of joy, whether physical, emotional, psychic, or intellectual, forms a bridge between the sharers which can be the basis for understanding much of what is not shared between them, and lessens the threat of their difference.

Another important way in which the erotic connection functions is the open and fearless underlining of my capacity for joy. In the way my body stretches to music and opens into response, hearkening to its deepest rhythms, so every level upon which I sense also opens to the erotically satisfying experience, whether it is dancing, building a bookcase, writing a poem, examining an idea.

That self-connection shared is a measure of the joy which I

know myself to be capable of feeling, a reminder of my capacity for feeling. And that deep and irreplaceable knowledge of my capacity for joy comes to demand from all of my life that it be lived within the knowledge that such satisfaction is possible, and does not have to be called marriage, or god, nor an afterlife.

This is one reason why the erotic is so feared, and so often relegated to the bedroom alone, when it is recognized at all. For once we begin to feel deeply all the aspects of our lives, we begin to demand from ourselves and from our lives' pursuits that they feel in accordance with that joy which we know ourselves to be capable of. Our erotic knowledge empowers us, becomes a lens through which we scrutinize all aspects of our existence, forcing ourselves to evaluate those aspects honestly in terms of their relative meaning within our lives. And this is a grave responsibility, projected from within each of us, not to settle for the convenient, the shoddy, the conventionally expected, or the merely safe.

During World War II, we bought sealed plastic packets of white, uncolored margarine, with a tiny, intense pellet of yellow coloring perched like a topaz just inside the clear skin of the bag. We would leave the margarine out for a while to soften, and then we would pinch the little pellet to break it inside the bag, releasing the rich yellowness into the soft pale mass of margarine. Then taking it carefully between our fingers, we would knead it gently back and forth, over and over, until the color had spread throughout the whole pound bag of margarine, leaving it thoroughly colored.

I find the erotic such a kernel within myself. When released from its intense and constrained pellet, it flows through and colors my life with a kind of energy that heightens and sensitizes and strengthens all my experience.

We have been raised to fear the yes within ourselves, our deepest cravings. For the demands of our released expectations lead us inevitably into actions which will help bring our lives into accordance with our needs, our knowledge, our desires. And the fear of our deepest cravings keeps them suspect, keeps us docile and loyal and obedient, and leads us to settle for or accept many facets of our oppression as women.

When we live outside ourselves, and by that I mean on external directives only, rather than from our internal knowledge and needs, when we live away from those erotic guides from within ourselves, then our lives are limited by external and alien forms, and we conform to the needs of a structure that is not based on human need, let alone an individual's. But when we begin to live from within outward, in touch with the power of the erotic within ourselves, and allowing that power to inform and illuminate our actions upon the world around us, then we begin to be responsible to ourselves in the deepest sense. For as we begin to recognize our deepest feelings, we begin to give up, of necessity, being satisfied with suffering and self-negation, and with the numbness which so often seems like their only alternative in our society. Our acts against oppression become integral with self, motivated and empowered from within.

In touch with the erotic, I become less willing to accept powerlessness, or those other supplied states of being which are not native to me, such as resignation, despair, self-effacement, depression, self-denial.

And yes, there is a hierarchy. There is a difference between painting a back fence and writing a poem, but only one of quantity. And there is, for me, no difference between writing a good poem and moving into sunlight against the body of a woman I love.

This brings me to the last consideration of the erotic. To share the power of each other's feelings is different from using another's feelings as we would use a Kleenex. And when we look the other way from our experience, erotic or otherwise, we use rather than share the feelings of those others who participate in the experience with us. And use without consent of the used is abuse.

In order to be utilized, our erotic feelings must be recognized. The need for sharing deep feeling is a human need. But within the European-American tradition, this need is satisfied by certain proscribed erotic comings together, and these occasions are almost always characterized by a simultaneous looking away, a pretense of calling them something else, whether a religion, a fit, mob violence, or even playing doctor. And this misnaming of the need and the deed gives rise to that distortion which results in pornography and obscenity—the abuse of feeling.

When we look away from the importance of the erotic in the development and sustenance of our power, or when we look away from ourselves as we satisfy our erotic needs in concert with others, we use each other as objects of satisfaction rather than share our joy in the satisfying, rather than make connection with our similarities and our differences. To refuse to be conscious of what we are feeling at any time, however comfortable that might seem, is to deny a large part of the experience, and to allow ourselves to be reduced to the pornographic, the abused, and the absurd.

The erotic cannot be felt secondhand. As a Black Lesbian Feminist, I have a particular feeling, knowledge, and understanding for those sisters with whom I have danced hard, played, or even fought. This deep participation has often been the forerunner for joint concerted actions not possible before.

But this erotic charge is not easily shared by women who continue to operate under an exclusively European-American, male tradition. I know it was not available to me when I was trying to adapt my consciousness to this mode of living and sensation.

Only now, I find more and more woman-identified women brave enought to risk sharing the erotic's electrical charge without having to look away, and without distorting the enormously powerful and creative nature of that exchange. Recognizing the power of the erotic within our lives can give us the energy to pursue genuine change within our world, rather than merely settling for a shift of characters in the same weary drama.

For not only do we touch our most profoundly creative source, but we do that which is female and self-affirming in the face of a racist, patriarchal, and antierotic society.

Letting Go with Love

MIRIAM
DECOSTA-WILLIS

Old folks used to say, "You don't know what you have till it's gone." What they rarely said, as footnote or clarification, is that for the bravest and smartest among us, loss can be transformed into rebirth. Life and love congeal so often around polarities and contradictions. The puzzling, often fumbling search for meaning embedded in the unfair or the painful can sometimes force us to tap into a mother lode of shimmering, unknown strength.

The death of a spouse or partner is a line of demarcation between a self molded with hands clasped and a self gasping for life and air alone. Marriages usually end as they began. The characteristics of the union imprint the moment of departure. Miriam DeCosta-Willis remembers her husband's dying. But most important, she shepherds us through the contours, rugged, slippery, delicate, and memorable, of what was a splendid love, discovered, renewed, and cherished unto the end.

Birth and death, the violent
rhythms of the passage into and
out of life.

Mine was
a childhood shrouded with images of death: uncles, dark and
gaunt, diminished by disease; aunts, silent and somber, in mourning black; women, coming and going, in whispers; bats and dead
birds littering Charleston streets after a raging hurricane. I learned
early that loss and pain and death are a part of the fabric of a richly
textured life, and that pain can sometimes underscore and intensify a deep and loving relationship.

I have two vivid images of my last years with A.*

May 1987. We are lying on the beach at Pointe du Bout,
where clouds move imperceptibly across a sky that changes from
pink to deep purple. I frame mental pictures, intent on remembering: palm trees etched against a darkening sky, sailboats an-
chored off shore, and seagulls in the distance. I hold this minute tight. We touch, but are lost in separate thoughts: memories
of the day—the slave cabins at Leyritz Plantation and the rain
forest resplendent with hibiscus and anthuriums—and anticipa-

---

*My husband's name was Archie Walter Willis, Jr., but people called him
"A.W.," while family members and close friends knew him as "A."

tion of the night, when we will make love as if for the last time.

Later that year. I am driving home through Memphis streets after a long faculty meeting. It is already dark and the deserted streets are wet from a late-fall rainstorm. I am cold and exhausted after a long and difficult day, when . . . my thoughts turn to A, home alone, waiting for me, sitting in the little room off our bedroom. I feel as though I am traveling through a long, dark tunnel at the end of which stands my husband, encircled by a warm, golden light. Transfigured, I move toward his light.

Joy in the midst of pain, for November was the beginning of the end. We recognized the signs—increased discomfort, weight loss, hoarseness, disorientation, and slurred speech—and we knew that the dark spots on the bone scan indicated that cancer had metastasized throughout his body. I held back tears when the doctor advised, "I would strongly urge you to get your affairs in order, Mr. Willis, because things might get quite difficult by the first of the year."

Actually, it had been a difficult two years. The discovery in August 1985 of a dark spot on the chest X ray, surgery two weeks later, and a one-month recuperation at home, followed by a long hiatus of apparent remission. But always, always was the uncertainty, the urgency to seize life, the feeling that every minute should be savored, relished. And then, in the spring of 1987, we learned that A's condition was terminal, that there were clusters of ring-shaped malignant tumors on both sides of his brain. That spring we prepared for his illness.

Now we had to get ready for his dying.

I say "we" because we confronted his illness and death together. I did the research: read books on cancer; ordered inspirational tapes; talked to doctors, pharmacists, and nutritionists; and called hospitals, cancer centers, and hotlines throughout the country. After I collected the data, we made decisions about treatment and care; we agreed, for example, that he would be cared for at home and that he would die at home. We also decided to be open and honest about his condition; too often, in Memphis at least, cancer patients and their families hide behind a veil of secrecy that requires so much emotional and psychic energy to maintain. It was very helpful for A to be able to talk about his illness. Openness and knowledge about the disease gave us a feeling, however tenuous, of control.

Our take-charge attitude sometimes had humorous consequences. When a battery of doctors visited A the day of his release from the hospital, we handed them a list of detailed questions that I had prepared. The first question read: "How soon can we have sex?" When the doctors responded with an embarrassed silence, we concluded that they could prevent dying but didn't understand much about "living." A month later, I turned to the oncologist after A's first bout with chemotherapy and asked, "What about sex?" The doctor mumbled, "Uh, maybe after six months. Er, sometimes it takes a year." He would be dismayed to know that we went right home and fell into each other's arms.

Although there were often passionless days and impotent nights, physical intimacy between us was very important because it affirmed who we were as individuals and how we connected as lovers. It reminded us that we were *alive*. Our lovemaking was an important ritual in the pattern of our lives; a quiet dinner, wine, bubblebath, candlelight, soft music, and gentle caresses were a prelude to a deeply satisfying physical communication. I was aware, however, of subtle changes in my feelings. After his surgery, I was more subdued, less enthusiastic about sex because I was afraid of hurting him, of pressing against the deep, painful scar that encircled his chest and back. And sometimes, in those last few months, when I held him in my arms and felt his thin, frail body against me, tears ran down my cheeks.

At age fifty, a time when I was facing changes—menopause; my daughters' marriages, divorces, and childbirths; and stressful problems at work—I had to deal with the illness and death of a man whom I loved deeply. Both of us had been married before, and so we brought to this second marriage of thirteen years all the tenderness, sensitivity, and understanding of a mature and responsible love. I think that A, a very sensitive and compassionate man, worried most about me when he became ill, and tried valiantly to prepare me, emotionally and financially, for life without him. An attorney, he had founded a mortgage company and was actively involved in downtown development, property renovation, and low-income housing, but he had spread himself too thin and had problems: tax bills, mounting debts, and an inadequate cash flow. He struggled desperately to keep the business going, while shoring up resources to support us during a protracted illness. We put everything on the table: our expenses, debts, wills, bank accounts, and property deeds. There were no hidden agendas, because we were in this thing together. I tried to assure him that I could support us, although my teaching position at a small, private, historically Black college did not pay much. "We can always sell the house and your car," I told him, concerned that worry would exacerbate his already precarious health. I wonder sometimes, in retrospect, how on earth two married people can mangage in a crisis without honesty and trust.

During his illness, we achieved an emotional intimacy that was more intense, more fulfilling, than any physical pleasure that we had ever experienced, primarily because A was so open and caring. I remember, particularly, the evenings we spent taping questions and answers about his work as a civil rights attorney, state legislator, and mortgage banker for the biography that I will write. There was a special magic in those hours we shared: A seated to my left in pajamas and bathrobe, his voice low and hoarse, recalling the people and events of his past; me scribbling notes in my pad while the tape recorder hummed between us.

We tried, even after that dark November, to live as normal a life as possible in spite of adjustments in our routine to schedule frequent visits to doctors and hospitals for tests, radiation treatment, and chemotherapy. I had to take him to work and friends would bring him home, because he was unable to drive. As late as February of 1988, though—five months before his death—A flew to Nashville to lobby for the Lorraine Civil Rights Museum and to attend a meeting of the Tennessee Racing Commission, community service for which he received no compensation. His determination to work in the face of fatigue, depression, constant pain, and severe weight loss (he weighed only 124 pounds by that time) was a lesson in living and dying with grace and dignity. Imperceptibly, however, the pace of our lives began to change, and we spent quiet days in slow motion. The two of us would sit outside on the patio for hours while he dozed in his chair and I looked out over the garden, feeling very much alone.

There were, though, moments to savor: presentation of an award to A by the governor, a testimonial banquet for him in November, the dedication of the A. W. Willis Bridge in December, Christmas dinner with our large extended family, a performance of *Peter Pan* with four of our grandchildren, and a portrait-taking session with our twenty-six-member family. Often we laughed together about the most awful things. In the oncologist's office, for example, he whispered, "Hey, Runt, looks like we landed on death row!"; and when, toward the end, we discussed his funeral plans, he chuckled, "I know you'll do it right. If not, I'll plan it my damn self." Once, we even cried together. While I was completing a paper to deliver in North Carolina the following day, A walked into my study and said, "I want to tell you good-bye," and then that strong, courageous man started crying. The idea of my leaving and the possibility of his dying alone frightened him, and he admitted, through tears, "I'm scared." (That was the only time in his long struggle with cancer that he ever expressed any fear; he told me that only two things worried him: unbearable pain and a long illness that left me in debt.) I put my arms around him, kissed him, and said, "I won't go. I'll stay here with you." Convinced that he would die that night, however, he didn't want to go to bed, so I took him in my arms and gently massaged his body. When he awoke the next morning, he said, "I made it through the night. The Lord has spared me one more time." Although I didn't have the solace of the church, A had a deep, abiding faith that sustained him through turbulent nights, when he dreamed that he couldn't wake up or witnessed his own funeral.

As the primary caregiver, I went through the same stages that A and other seriously ill people experienced: disbelief, denial, shock, fear, anger, depression, rage, and a pain so deep that at times I could not breathe or even think straight. After the meeting with the doctor in November, I wrote in my journal:

> I thought I had prepared myself emotionally for every eventuality, but with each onslaught of the disease I ache and am in such pain. I feel as if someone is squeezing my chest, as if there is a heavy weight pressing me down and sapping my energy.

Pain seeped through the cracks of my carefully constructed wall, a protective wall that I built up over months of reading, for I always turned to books for solace, comfort, and escape, aware that the words of others could help me through traumatic experiences. Books like Audre Lorde's *The Cancer Journals,* Gerda Lerner's *A Death of One's Own,* and Elisabeth Kübler-Ross's *On Death and Dying* helped me understand what A was going through; relaxation tapes—waterfalls, rain forests, and seashores—calmed my nerves; and Louise Hays's self-healing tapes alleviated my depression. Through creative visualization, I began to rehearse my life without A, creating an imaginary future in another place with new friends and a different lifestyle.

And I tried, really tried, to take care of myself, first, because A depended on me, and second, because I needed good health to cope with his illness and, later, to make a new life without him. After learning that the illness was terminal, I joined a health-and-fitness center, and the following spring, during the really rough period, I started a diet program and lost twenty-five pounds. Eating right and exercising gave me a feeling of control in a situation that was very hard for me, a highly structured person, to deal with.

In spite of my carefully constructed defenses, there were times when I slipped over the edge. I was often tired—no, exhausted—because I got very little sleep, particularly during that last spring when A was so agitated and restless. He would get up eight or ten times during the night, turn on the lights, stumble around, and cough loudly. Sometimes, when he awakened at 2 A.M., unable to sleep because of pain or depression, I would listen while he talked about his plans for low-income housing or for the Lorraine Civil Rights Museum, but then I couldn't go back to sleep. I was depressed and tense one day, irritable and nervous the next. Frequently, I had difficulty concentrating, which was devastating for my work. That year, I designed an honors program for which I had to write grant proposals, and I taught the first interdisciplinary honors course, which included guest lectures, visits to cultural events, and trips to conferences—all of which taxed my energy and creativity. Somehow, I muddled through, fearing that I would never write again because my life-force was ebbing away.

At times I was impatient or sharp with A. Once, when I was very tired and had a bad cold, I told him, "I'm so tired of talking about cancer. I just can't take it any longer. I'm doing the best I can, but I'm under a lot of stress too." I felt so ashamed of myself, a few days later, when I heard him tell his youngest daughter how supportive I'd been, that he couldn't have made it without me. I tried so hard to hold my sharp tongue in check, but occasionally I let loose. The month before I started losing weight, he teased, "You sure are getting fat," and I shot back, "But *I'm* healthy!" That was really hitting below the belt, but I was feeling so bad about myself; I looked dumpy and matronly, and I had terrible bags under my eyes.

The hardest part was dealing with powerful contradictory impulses: attraction to a man I deeply loved, but aversion to his wasted, scarred, sickly body; desire to spend time with him, but feeling trapped; comfort in having people around, while longing for privacy and time alone; concern about his care, but fear for my future. Occasionally, I felt guilty or ashamed of those very human feelings, but I was doing the best that I could to care for and nurture my husband, while trying to hold on to my own sanity. My journal was an important tool in struggling with anxiety, ambivalence, and contradictory feelings. Sometimes it was hard to confront the ugly part of me. I thought how much easier it is, so much less painful, to stand at the periphery of life—to avoid too much intimacy with others, to treat the surface realities, and to eschew deep reflection on darker feelings: shame, guilt, anger, and self-loathing. Three months before A's death, I wrote in my journal:

> All day I was tense and numb, the result no doubt of depression. I felt a little like I did last April—tired, removed from everything, despondent. I felt as if the walls were closing in on me. I didn't want to come home; I just wanted to run away.

No, I didn't run away, but I did, on occasion, escape, physically and psychologically. I would slip off from work in the afternoon to view a foreign film or, if friends came to visit A, head for the park with a book, blanket, and sandwich in hand. Lying under dogwood trees beside the lake, I found the peace and serenity to take me through another week. One of my coping mechanisms is to withdraw into myself, my work, my own interests, and so, when things got rough, I found myself starting to distance myself psychologically from my husband and his illness.

Those last few months were an emotional roller coaster ride because A began to have mood swings, which the doctor had warned us about; he became delusional and, once or twice, hostile. When he was no longer able to go to the office, he began to do things around the house because he needed to feel like a functioning human being; he would dig up the flowers, chop up garbage to cook, and leave the broiler on all day. I couldn't leave him alone after that. One night, I woke up to find him standing over me in the dark, asking where his guns were because he had to shoot someone. Another night, he walked up to the bed and said, "I'm going to take you with me." I jumped up and screamed, "The hell you are!" I have to smile about those incidents now, but they were very unsettling at the time. I often had to remind myself that cancer, particularly brain tumors, had changed the man I loved. After an especially difficult day, when I crawled into bed, he accused me of not caring about him, of being wrapped up in

myself, of caring more about my women friends. Later, he turned
to my son and said very calmly, "Your mother's a lesbian," probably because he overheard me laughing and talking with friends—
my primary outlet during that period of confinement. The next
day, I wrote in my journal, "He looked at me last night with such
hatred. Where did the love go?"

That brief phase was followed by a period of tremendous anxiety and dependence on me; he fretted when I left home, called
frequently, and summoned me out of classes and meetings. Although I had a woman to stay with him while I was in class, I
took care of him when I came home: bathed, shaved, and dressed
him; massaged him with lotion; watched movies with him at
night. In early June, when I tried to help him up out of his chair,
he collapsed to the floor and I had to leave him there, resting on a
pillow and covered with a blanket, until morning, when I called
our son-in-law to help me get him up. When his condition wors-
ened and he became completely bedridden, I hired nurses. The
doctor offered to hospitalize him after the situation became difficult for me, but I think that hospitals too often function like
nursing homes—to warehouse the sick and shield the family from
the harsher realities of sickness and dying. I wanted to keep A at
home, where we could share his last days, the children and grandchildren could visit him, and he could die peacefully, surrounded
by loved ones.

But the world was too much with me those last weeks: nurses
on eight-hour shifts, nine grown children (his and mine) chatting
until late at night, kids running through the house, and daughters
sprawled across our bed. Most days, we had several visitors, but
one Sunday I counted twenty-six people, playing basketball outside, lounging around the pool, opening the refrigerator, and in-
vading my private space—my study. That was the place where I
went to cry *alone,* because I had been taught by stoic parents to
suffer in silence, never complaining or feeling sorry for myself.
Now I didn't even have solitude for my private pain.

Eventually, I converted our bedroom into a sickroom: set up a
hospital bed, ordered an oxygen tank, bought medical supplies,

replaced the perfume bottles on my dresser with codeine tablets and liquid morphine. Twice, I took him to the hospital for blood transfusions, while my stepdaughter and I sat with him, talking, reading, and writing letters. Their father's illness created a close bond between me and A's five children by a previous marriage, and I called them often for advice, help, and support.

One afternoon in mid-July, while my sister-in-law and I were talking in my study, the nurse came down the hall and said, "I think Mr. Willis has gone." I walked into our room, bent down, and whispered in his ear, "I love you. I'll miss you."

I used to tell my best friend, "I'm so lucky," but she would smile and say, "No, you're blessed." Indeed, I have been truly blessed to have known and loved a man like A, to have shared a life with him, and to have accompanied him on his final rite of passage. Those last three years were a gift.

Now, when I close my eyes and images of uncles and widowed aunts flicker before me—men who died and women who cared for them—I understand the meaning of love and the profound connection between life and death.

A New Shower Massage,

Phone Sex,

and Separation

TINA
MCELROY ANSA

When I started asking women to write about love, men, and sex, frankly I didn't know what my sisters would conclude either collectively or individually. What surprised me was that nobody wanted to write just about SEX. Everybody preferred to dive headfirst into the whole stew, stirring up a brew that blended emotions and passion into a tasty concoction.

Women spent a lot of time in the seventies and early eighties discovering and perfecting orgasms, learning the proper names and pronunciation for the parts of our genitalia we weren't taught in health classes (a cover in the fifties for watered-down sex ed). And we discovered sex could be a game, a toy, a commitment, a passion, a pastime, a source of guilt (we hadn't eradicated that completely), a source of infections, a way to be grown up, pretend we were, a way to catch a man, lose a man, keep a man (or woman). We found sex everywhere.

Adjusting to a commuter marriage, Tina McElroy Ansa found that sex, sexuality, and intimacy infused countless regions of her relationship with her husband. What do sex, love, fidelity mean when you live in one city and your mate in another? A solid monogamous union can, in the right hands, be a tool for sculpting the most exciting treasures from the materiel of the known, the established, the safe and secure. A good marriage, fashioned together or apart, comes with its own set of firecrackers that go off when needed.

When I made love for the first time, I chose the man, the place, the time (of day and of the month), and the pea-green empire nightgown I wore for the occasion.

The act of intercourse occurred about a month before my twenty-second birthday on a night after a seductive evening with the most intelligent, decent, wittiest man I had met at that time whose mouth I wanted to explore. I planned the dinner menu, the "moment," the quotes, the timing (he was scheduled to move back to his hometown in a few weeks to take a new job), the music.

As an older virgin, I had decided early on not to hand my sexuality to just any pimply-faced boy with hot hands and breath in the backseat of his parents' car. Instead, I had consciously decided to control and deal with my sexuality on my own terms.

What my sexuality meant to me at that time was my virginity. It was not something that I guarded as if I were a vestal virgin. But my virginity had never been for me what some of my girlfriends considered it to be: a burden, an onerous inconvenience that needed to be unloaded so you could get on with your life. For years, I had listened with horror as friends related tales of their first times, replete with rushed fumbling of hands on zippers and snaps and buttons in uncomfortable spaces, parents bursting in at the climactic moment, days afterward spent in fervent prayer for the next anticipated menstrual flow. I planned to have none of that.

It had not escaped me that by dint of my date of birth in the late forties and concomitant shifts in our society (the sexual revolution, the women's movement, the civil rights movement/freedom movement, wide use of the birth control pill), I was among the first generation of American women, and especially African-American women, with such a wide range of tools of sexual empowerment (unheard-of opportunities in career choice, a college education, varied methods of birth control, growth in single households). And I felt a definite but unvoiced obligation to use these vehicles. If not for myself and my future, then at least for all those black women who went into the sexual minefield before me unarmed with these weapons.

For my first time, I was determined not to pick a backseat fumbler, but a more experienced, sensitive man. I was not about to be rushed. I owned the bed and paid the rent each month on the house in which it stood. I had gone to my gynecologist a while before for birth control. And I had all night.

That first time was nearly perfect, mostly, I figured, because it was what *I* wanted in the way *I* wanted it. And consciously and subconsciously, that first time set the pattern of my seminal sexual life.

As a single woman in the seventies with a well-paying, interesting job, I felt that sexual freedom was one of the prerogatives of my society and times. On one weekend visit to my mother's house when my sister and I were both single, my sister suddenly remembered something in the middle of a mother-daughters conversation and jumped up to get her purse. Not giving it a thought, she sat down and pulled out her yellow packet of birth control pills, popped one out and took it.

"Ohh," I said, remembering too, and got up to do the same thing.

Our mother sat silently watching us a moment, then said, "Ya'll don't have no respect for me." Her voice was chiding, but she couldn't hide the tinge of respect she had for us for taking care of ourselves, being free, single women—everything she had worked so hard to allow and empower us to be.

I was grateful for the freedom and used it. In a pre–AIDS–aware society, I chose my partners, initiated and ended relationships and encounters with an eye to pleasure, mutual fulfillment, curiosity, and affection. Hurt no one else with your screwing was certainly part of my motto. But foremost, get what you want and don't hurt yourself. In my twenties, I was not looking for a long-term relationship, just satisfaction.

When I found the man I did love and want to make a commitment to, I was surprised that so special a man could have fallen in my path. We got married before I turned thirty.

Certainly, Jonee' and I discussed sexuality before and after our marriage. Mostly we talked about monogamy and without question settled on it. I was happy and safe and secure in the relationship. We were both artists, both a little crazy, and we loved each other more than anything in the world (other than our art). Attractive, sexy, interesting people certainly came into our lives, but we discovered that sexual satisfaction in a long-term relationship is a happy and comfortable place to be.

In an era in which black women lamented the dearth of "good" available black men in every place from the beauty shop to contemporary literature and film, I figured I was set.

Then, the man I had lived with, loved, and, as important, had sex with for fourteen years moved three thousand miles away to attend film school for two years.

His acceptance as a Cinematography Fellow at the American Film Institute in Los Angeles, a longed-for blessing, began a period in my life in which I had to grapple with questions, situations, and yearnings that I thought I had long ago solved.

Suddenly, in my forties, I felt as if my sexuality had been snatched from me when my sexual partner left.

Our separation, which still continues now from time to time, began a journey for me through that sexual minefield I thought I had traversed cunningly and safely years before. Now, I found I had to explore exactly what my sexuality meant to my life and identity, what to *do* with it while my man was away for long periods of time, who I let into my bubble of sexuality and how that impacted on my marriage and my feelings for my husband. Most important, I learned how much sex is *about* copulation and how much sex is about something else: jealousy, trust, sharing, assurance, love.

The space that a lover leaves in your life and your household is even deeper and broader when you know this is not a short-term deal.

After a few months, I discovered that it wasn't the length of our separations that impacted most heavily on our feeling of sexual deprivation. (At one point, we didn't see each other for six months.) It was the timing of our separations. As the original Ms. Want It When I Want It, I found that our separations and the attendant lack of sex made my emotions range from self-pity to anger.

But matters quickly turned from the abstract and emotional to the concrete when I brought up the subject of sexual fulfillment in times of separation to a woman who had been conducting a successful long-distance marriage for some time. "Well, Girl," the peripatetic scholar advised me, "you're gonna have to get heavy into some phone sex with your man while he's away."

"Phone sex???"

"Yeah, phone sex!" I could almost hear her add to herself, "Miss Thing!"

"Like fucking over the phone? Won't the operators be listening."

"Yeah, probably," she said.

I began to learn the limits of my sexual liberality. I began to feel old. In my single, nonmonogamous days, I'm sure, I would not have even *needed* the suggestion about phone sex, let alone felt hesitant about doing it.

But a contented sex life with one partner, I discovered, makes one less open to new ideas, less adventurous, less likely to work without a net. And in the absence of the security of my partner there with me, I felt vulnerable and, yes, shy fucking on the phone.

Other avenues had to be explored, since I had also discovered that one cannot fuck enough in a two-week visit to hold one over for the next six months. And Jonee' and I had both discovered separation not only heightens one's sexual appetite, but also, apparently, one's sexual appeal.

We discussed how it seemed that suddenly, outrageously, we were more attractive, seductive, alluring than we had been when we were together. More people were coming on to us than we ever remembered happening when we were together. We wondered if we, unconsciously, wore signs that proclaimed I'M HORNY AS HELL AND MY MAN/MY WOMAN IS LIVING THOUSANDS OF MILES AWAY.

This new sexual allure brought with it not only possibilities of easing the problem, but also new considerations. Now, I found I had to make conscious decisions about my sexuality and my choices on sexual involvement. I could not even flirt as casually as before without considering the implications, because I could no longer say, when I'd had enough, "Well, so long, Fella. Gotta go. My old man's waiting at home." Because he wasn't and the weight of the decision of whether or not to *go home* fell on me. With Jonee' away, it was totally my responsibility whether dinner with a new male acquaintance on the road or at home constituted a "date," and my responsibility to let him know what the situation was.

Making these decisions on a regular basis, I found, changes one. My choice of lover and marriage partner was no longer a decision I made years ago and now just comfortably followed. Now, with my husband away, it was a choice I had to make over and over again, with new and old acquaintances. It was a choice that I was now called upon to announce, explain, defend, and justify, to myself as well as to others. I had to weigh seriously faithfulness, honesty, and love against the body and spirit of a gorgeous twenty-two-year-old grad student who laughed ingenuously at the idea of not having the pleasure of each other for the afternoon "just because you're married."

It also meant having to hear stories (over the phone) from Jonee' in Hollywood of meeting his favorite actress and getting invited repeatedly to a "home-cooked meal."

What's up with that? I wanted to know. Sex is also about jealousy.

The new element of more available sex in our lives had its impact on both of us. We decided on continuing to strive for monogamy, but without saying a word to me, Jonee' did check out the bathtub shower head and replaced it with a new shower massager before he left town again.

Between the shower massager, the possibility of me working my way up to phone sex, fantasies, titillating stories from my friends about their sexual exploits, and repeated reminders that this separation was not going to last forever, I was once again beginning to feel pretty well covered during our separations.

But it wasn't long before I began to feel again the lacuna that my man's absence left. It was not just the sexual act that I missed. I could get off by myself, I had *that* down pat. And it wasn't totally that I missed sex with the man that I loved.

My longing was rooted more in intimacy. It was not about a vibrator and sexual satisfaction as much as it was about the yearning for a closeness and the assurance of another person's love, about a face-to-face talk about sex or a writing assignment or needed car repair that ends not in the click of the phone, but in the holding of hands or the meeting of eyes or a slap or squeeze of the knee or the slam of a door.

When our reunions started beginning not with a rushed tearing off of clothes but with a breathless question or announcement, I knew to take notice. "Wait till you hear who showed up on my movie set . . ." or "I can't wait for you to smell the ginger lily blooming" were as important to our relationship as "Hey, do me right now!" because only he and I know how he struggled to be a filmmaker and because he and I are the only ones who give a damn that the intoxicatingly fragrant ginger lily was blooming under our bedroom window again.

In the absence of steady sex, other sensual feelings seemed to come to the forefront. Through our separation, we discovered the sensuality present in eating a simple well-prepared meal together, drinking too much wine, remembering what it feels like to be giddy together. And what it feels like to be quiet together.

Early one sultry evening in late summer on one of Jonee's trips home, we went for a walk along the beach to cool off. We strolled awhile in silence, our bare shoulders brushing from time to time. When we reached the lighthouse, we both stopped and looked out to sea in search of the dolphins we both knew circled and fed on fat mullet there. Finding none there, Jonee' looked at me with a familiar smile and said, "Um, must be past dinnertime." Then, we walked on, never having mentioned dolphins, mullet, or UN-SPOKEN rituals.

I had not fully realized until our separation that we had over the years built this tower of intimacy that had as its foundation other building blocks as strong as sex.

Through our times together and apart I began to see the examples of our intimacy that had nothing to do with sex. I began to see the intimacy of conversation we shared whether the topic was personal, political, the garden, our work, gossip, the island where we live, or sexual. Or the intimacy of preparing a meal together in the kitchen and, as if we had rehearsed it, not bumping into each other.

Sometimes, I now notice that I wake in the morning when Jonee' is in town and am amused that the sight of him lying next to me in our bed, not hundreds or thousands of miles away, takes my breath away. The very nearness of him makes my heart race as if I'd experienced an orgasm. The awareness of the intimacy of our relationship whether we are together or not has touched us and bonded us in a way that constant companionship never did. An appreciation of the intimacy of marriage, of a long-term relationship, grew from our separation and our lack of sex together.

Of course, his presence at home and the heightened sense of intimacy in our relationship do intensify the longing for him when he is away, but it is almost a sweet longing now. Not frantic or angry or self-pitying.

The sexual and spiritual journey that began three years ago

when Jonee' left for Hollywood and that continues as we now both travel around the country with our work has been a revelation. I discovered that my sexuality certainly wasn't snatched from me when my lover left the vicinity. Rather, it was given back to me, opened up and enriched by our separation. My sexuality now is there for me to deal with actively, to be responsible for and to enjoy.

Walking

in My Mother's Footsteps

to Love

MARITA GOLDEN

My parents were the first lovers whose drama I saw unfold. I have battled with the legacy of romantic and sexual love they shaped together and bequeathed to me, one riddled with anguish, regret and reconciliation. Much of my adult life has been spent unlearning the expectations, resisting the responses, challenging the manner in which my parents loved one another. But when I gazed closely, almost clinically, at what I learned most painfully and therefore most totally from the man and woman who gave me life and faith in myself, I discovered lessons I can hold on to, signposts I dare not ignore.

Everything I have learned about love, I learned from my mother. For it is mothers who bend, twist, flex, and break most dramatically before our uninitiated eyes. Fathers bear, conceal, inflict, sometimes vanish, so the mythology of domestic union tells us. But mothers absorb, accept, give in, all to tutor daughters in the syntax, the grammar of yearning and love.

My mother, Beatrice Lee Reid, fled poverty and Greensboro, North Carolina, in the late twenties, leaving an ex-husband behind. I learned of this prior husband offhandedly, in passing, a secret hoarded until I was nearly twenty. She arrived in Washington, D.C., radiant, ambitious, and subsequently married two more men. The first of the two, Mr. Robinson, was benevolent, and possessed of a heart he swore was designed only to love my mother. But Mr. Harold Robinson, haunted by childhood demons and doubts, was an alcoholic who too often sank to the status of drunk. And while in the grip of such anguish, he drove away the woman that in his irregular moments of lucidity and confidence, he almost perfectly loved.

Francis Sherman Golden was my mother's third husband. He was steel-willed and eager to control the small fortune my mother had gained through gambling and hard work. Even more than he wanted to love Beatrice Lee Reid, Francis Sherman Golden longed to conquer and absorb her will. To my mother he must have seemed as large as Mr. Robinson appeared small. Francis Sherman Golden was my father.

It is only now, inside the fluid boundaries of a good, loving marriage, that I can face and recompose the lessons my mother taught me about love. Her legacy to me is stark and contradictory. I watched the drama of my parents' turbulent, tortured union and learned that it isn't love unless it hurts.

My parents' marriage was a symphony of passion and extremes. Both my parents were gamblers. They played the numbers and won often. I remember the trips to Raleigh's, a downtown department store where in the wake of a big winning, my father would stand before the three-way mirror, peacock proud, being measured by a white salesman for a half dozen tailor-made suits. I remember the black Lincoln Continental he bought once and how it sat, sleek and somehow fitting, before our three-story rooming house until it was repossessed three months later.

My parents gambled with their emotions too, perfecting arctic silences, filling the house with blasts of recrimination and accusation that echoed long into the night, crawling beneath my bedroom door and living inside my dreams. My father regularly stalked out of the house bags in hand, only to return a week later, my mother's arms greeting him with trembling and faith.

In the last, most awful years of this marriage I sometimes accompanied my mother on furtive, yet somehow sacred visits to Mr. Robinson. In his cramped, tiny basement apartment they sat and talked, openly, affection warming each word, the way I rarely saw my mother talk with my father. In the midst of what I now know was an act of mutual courage, I saw conversation turn into a sensual, life-giving force. I watched my mother talk to her ex-husband and learned that love is sometimes remarkably straightforward and that love is feeling safe.

Parents render lessons about love in subversive, ironic ways. My father often took me with him when he visited the women my mother accused him of having as lovers. These women doted on me, bribed me with candy and other treats, installing me in the kitchen or in the living room before their nineteen-inch black-and-white TVs, while they catered to my father, my presence giving them one more reason to love him. These women taught me nothing, for I was too ashamed of my father to look at them.

But when I went with my mother to visit Mr. Robinson, silver-haired, so light-skinned he had sometimes passed for white before marrying my caramel-colored mother, I saw a man ravaged by alcohol and other demons who nonetheless provoked in my mother a loyalty and compassion my father seemed not to need. My mother and Mr. Robinson sat before me creating a vocabulary grounded in forgiveness, which is the real foundation of love.

Francis Sherman Golden was a powerful antidote to the disappointment my mother must have felt in the wake of her break with Mr. Robinson. Once she hinted at the sexual reawakening my father inspired when they met in the first months after she left Mr. Robinson. My mother was a marvelously feminine, sexually confident woman who met more than her match in my father. They were combustible and electric together; this is what my mother meant when she told me once that when she got up in the mornings, my father made her feel as if she could tear up the house and put it back together again. But during the years of their marriage they never shaped a language to escort them from the horizontal to the vertical, from passion to navigating gracefully through the commonplace, the mundane.

I've often wondered what my mother thought about love. How she defined it. What had HER mother told her of its power? Its dangers? These are the questions daughters are taught not to ask openly. Questions mothers answer by accident with practiced obliqueness.

The most definitive anecdote I recall about my maternal grandmother is the time, according to family legend, that she got so angry with her husband that she decided for the rest of their marriage to sleep on her side of the bed, separated from him so far that over the years the mattress "caved in," forming a line of demarcation between my grandmother's rigid, unforgiving will and my grandfather, beaten into respect and acquiescence.

This is the story that in family lore, told with chagrined laugh-

ter and embarrassment, and awe at the staunchness of my grandmother, is meant to be a commentary on marriage and love. And
if my mother spoke to me of love obliquely, and often in code,
her mother spoke to her of love, I am sure, not at all.

The deaths of my parents, a year and a half apart, as I was
completing college, have given them to me, in the years that have
passed, truer, more clearly, than they existed in life. I loved them
when they lived. In the aftermath of their deaths I have tried to
infuse love with perception. They have transcended the limiting
designation of mother/father. My own faltering, reckless, sometimes wise attempts at loving men have imbued me with an empa-
thy for how hard it was for them to do what they did—raise me
with love, even when the love they felt for one another was so
fragile and so frequently mocked their best intentions.

Because I now possess my own personal history of love failed
and remade, marriage tried and reshaped, I recall my parents
through the telescope of a memory whose lens is finally clear,
magnifying, minimizing, but honing them into a sharper image of
who they really were. I know now that my mother must have
been irresistible to my father. When he met her she was just past
forty, a Black woman as restless, hungry for life as he. She had
propelled herself from domestic worker to property owner, and
her personal charisma rivaled his own, hovering around her like
some expensive yet subtle perfume enhanced by her skin. I am the
age now my mother was when she met my father, so I know how
ripe she was, how unquenchable was her thirst for fulfillment. She
had proved herself to herself. But she wanted more.

I like to think that there must have been periods of content-
ment, satisfaction, for my mother with my father. I just don't
recall those times as vividly as I remember the pain.

I rarely saw my parents kiss, but I saw them fight more than I
care to remember. The fights were the sorrowful, exhausted last-
ditch efforts of two intelligent people for whom words simply did
not work. These were not the kinds of physical battles that black-
ened eyes, or sparked blood from broken, peeling skin, or produced maimed limbs. Rather, they were carefully choreographed

dances of rage, as articulate in their own way as a blast of oratory. In the most vivid, awful memory I am eight years old and waking from a nap on the sofa one evening. I had been awakened by muffled yet clearly audible groans and a thudding, thumping sound. I woke up, I remember, slowly, unwillingly, for somewhere buried in my consciousness was knowledge of what I would see once I opened my eyes. My father was pushing my mother, a sturdy, buxom woman, dressed, I remember even now, in a fashionable print dress, against the flowered-wallpapered living room walls, again and again. There were no fists, no slaps, just a continual pushing, he of her, against the wall, as if to pin her there and capture or extinguish the source of her resistance, and her continued pushing against him. I sat on the sofa immobilized, shamed, afraid, hating, loving them both, willing myself to disappear, willing my body to move, but not moving because I'd never been able to stop them before. Finally in my imagination I transported myself out of the room, but was still racked by guilt because I did not try to stop them.

What I remember most is that my mother, in those trysts of violence, always gave as good as she got. I remember too that my father, even in anger, never unleashed the full force of his physical power. But mostly I remember that my mother refused to back down.

As seemingly required in the aftermath of the most shameful acts, in the days following the fights we each conspired to obliterate it from memory. Words had failed my parents then. How could they function for them now? At eight, I was too obedient, too well trained, forgiving the burden my parents' marital incompetence imposed on me, and said nothing as well. I think we all believed if nothing was said, maybe nothing had really happened.

My mother left my father in 1963 and died eight years later. She waited too long to leave. And she never retrieved what was good about her life before she met my father. The only thing she'd gained from their thirteen years together was me. She always told me I was more than worth it.

And when my mother left my father, it wasn't because of the

fights. How I wish it had been. But rather, my mother left because my father had gambled away all but one of her houses and severely reduced her financial autonomy. My father was a hustler, con artist, and gambler whose prowess with women was, within his circle of friends, nearly legendary. And the question that haunts me the deeper I dig into the terrain of my own life as a woman is, How did my mother, strong-willed, self-possessed, let my father steal her life like a ruthless, petty thief? Neither my heart nor my intellect will accept love as the answer though I, like my mother have at times forsaken judgment and prudence for what I thought love would assure. Years after her death, one of my mother's oldest friends told me, "Bea just couldn't say no to your father when he asked her for money. She told me sometimes she'd go out and buy something, anything, just so she wouldn't have to give the money to your father. Because if he asked her for it, it was his."

I wish she'd left him because of the fights. Since she stayed so long, I learned that a woman could, if she was strong enough emotionally, stand up, over and over, to a fight with a man. This is a cruel, double-edged lesson to learn. Still, I swore I'd never let a man hit me. When my first husband did, I left him to keep it from happening again. Yet, several years later I found myself trapped in the twilight zone of a relationship much like my parents', where honorable, openhearted, intimate speech was an impossibility.

With this man I played out the same script my parents had acted out so well. Like my parents, though much less frequently, we fought because we could not talk, struck out because we couldn't truly love. Like my mother, I gave as good as I got. Like my father, he fought me not to hurt me but to win psychological submission. If the memory of my inaction in the face of my parents' violence haunts me from childhood, the memory of the righteous, transforming, physically ennobling power of anger coursing through my veins and urging me to meet each shove of his with a shove of my own, to challenge each grip, each hold as though my life depended on it, is indelible in present memory. I fought back, forgetting shame, fear, determined like my mother that I would not be subdued. Maybe he WAS a man. But I was a WOMAN. It was the feel of my son tugging at my skirt in the middle of one of these battles that landed a blow more stunning than any my lover could. It was the wounds taking shape in my sons eyes as he gazed at this man and me as if we were strangers he feared that brought me down for the count. No man has hit me since. No man ever will.

My mother taught me to leave. She also taught me to stay. How does a mother talk to her daughter about the feel of her husband's fist against her cheek? About the corrupt, aching silence in darkened bedrooms in the aftermath? Is there a language for this? My mother never found one for me.

Like my mother, in my adult life, I mastered the grand exit, the final, cataclysmic leave-taking that was combination kiss-my-behind and a romantic heroine's spine-straight stride into the future just beyond the horizon.

My mother left home and walked away from three husbands, exiling herself each time, she thought, from unhappiness and the grip of someone else's fingers around the neck of her hopes. No, she didn't find nirvana on the other side of the closed door. But leaving is no guarantee of anything more than that you're taking yourself with you.

When my mother left my father, she did it as easily, as sublimely, as going for a Sunday drive. After the years of arguments, the fights, the test of wills, she was too exhausted, I imagine, to leave with anything other than grace and forbearance. I entered the house after school that afternoon and she told me simply, "We're leaving your father." This was the statement I had spent much of my childhood dreading, waiting to hear, watching it take shape in the bickering, the sniping, and the increasing absence of affection. Wordlessly, obediently, I followed my mother's instructions to pack my clothes in a suitcase. I was wordless, obedient, because I was as exhausted and as numb as my mother, as emotionally drained, my loyalties ravaged and battered by a father I still adored and a mother I loved and trusted despite the debris that had become her life.

That day my mother taught me that you CAN leave, it is never too late to do that. The rooming houses she'd cherished were now gone. And she would live her remaining years sorely regretting what she had lost. So, maybe sometimes it is too late to leave, too late for the leaving to matter. But my mother would say, leave anyway.

So, when I had to, I could leave a man when it was over because I had witnessed my mother say goodbye to my father when nothing was left.

But in the years that followed, when my father became a visitor in our tiny city-subsidized apartment, and my parents became, miraculously, friends, my mother stoked and encouraged my loyalty and love of my father despite their past, perhaps because of it. She never allowed me to do anything less than honor my father.

My mother exiled herself from three men whose names and legacies she had carried. With Mr. Robinson and my father, I watched her shape, in the aftermath of her flight, some facsimile of emotional equity, find the flickers of grace and charity that had sometimes activated even the most impenetrable moments of shared doubt and mistrust. I don't know what compelled my mother to shape with these men so steadfastly, after marriage, what had been resistant and foreign when she was bound to them by love and law. Was marriage too confining a concept for Beatrice Lee Reid? Did she require in the end autonomy and the love of a man? Neither my father nor Mr. Robinson possessed the emotional integration, the proper mix of strength and vulnerability, my mother required. But the evidence, as I sift through the remnants of my mother's life, like searching for a ghost, reveals that my mother was a woman of extremes whose love thrived somehow on the off-center, the slightly distorted.

My surrogate aunt, one of my mother's oldest friends, who witnessed my mother's life up close, who saw her fall for Mr.

Robinson and come under the spell of my father, told me that one evening when she sat with my mother bemoaning the aftermath of a disappointing love affair, she swore, "No more men. Never again." My mother looked at her across the table, laughed and countered, "Well, there's always gonna be somebody's feet up under my table." This is a declaration of independence and a recognition of the necessity of mating, sex, and love. That "somebody" would be sitting at MY MOTHER's table, not his own, yet they would be there because she wanted and needed them to be. Was my mother's need to control more noble than my father's impulse to do the same? Did my mother want a man she could respect or one she could master? I don't know, and because I loved my mother so much I strive even while looking back to see her fully dimensional, without apology. She would offer no excuses for her choices, for she knew answers were not solutions, but a way to get from one day to the next. "Your mother was her own women in the end," my aunt concluded. "She loved Mr. Robinson and your father, but Mr. Robinson wasn't strong enough to hold her. Your father's strength came up against hers and she wouldn't give in."

When I left my first husband and suffered several years of bitter, guilty estrangement, because I am my mother's daughter there came a time when I had to give my son back his father, as my mother had given me mine. Though my son and his father are separated by a continent, I fan the flames of their father/son love, retrieved, in time, I found. It is never too late to claim lineage, bones and blood. My mother taught me to leave, to stay, and to forgive.

I fell in love with and married the man who is my husband now because he is not afraid to feel or express affection. I love him because he can TELL me what he needs and wants. My husband is as addicted to language, its possibilities, its power, as am I. And I fell in love with his ability to talk, was seduced by his skillful obliteration of the remembered, never forgotten silences of my parents' marriage and my first. My mother taught me how to find this man, and what to do once I had him. For in her sojourns back to Mr. Robinson she dramatized for me the excitement, the thrill of a man and woman sitting together, talking quietly, sometimes saying nothing verbally, allowing a gaze, a touch, to articulate what was too monumental and fragile to be said. Often it was my mother talking the most, and I saw Mr. Robinson listen, his dull, weathered demeanor transformed, flushed by the import of my mother's words. My mother was teaching me that love is talking and it is listening too.

Certainly, I would have wished more happiness for my mother. But while I witnessed her marriage to my father, I was a spectator, biased and with vested interests. I was not resident inside the skin of their feelings, I could hear their voices but not always perfectly translate the text. Perhaps the respect they accorded one another in the end was a kind of love, the one they had been journeying toward all along.

One February afternoon in 1971, my mother suffered a cerebral hemorrhage from which she ultimately died six months later. She was sixty-three years old. The day before the stroke she had spent the afternoon with her special "man friend," who lived several blocks from our apartment. When she entered the apartment that afternoon, some intangible aura of satisfaction blossoming around her, her movements energized and quick, I knew she had had sex. I could tell, for I was twenty-one and had come home from the arms of my boyfriend—my body, my senses humming the same splendid tune. But I was ambivalent, sometimes downright hostile to the idea of my mother, arthritic, sometimes forgetful, having an affair with a man; my mother, gray-haired, unmarried, having sex. But my mother had decided that she would live until she died. Throughout her life, every exit, every stand taken, every act of loyalty, every transgression forgotten, had stitched another panel in this belief. My mother lived and loved until she died. I am her daughter and so will I.

Sleeping with
the Enemy

AUDREY EDWARDS

The sturdy construct of racism has never managed to quell sexual desire or the blossoming of affection between men and women ruled by law and custom outside the borders of each other's imagination. In the Black community, the white man as symbol of power, the white woman as trophy have long activated the hidden longings only discussed in anger, or dredged up as proof of racial betrayal.

Audrey Edwards remembers white men she has loved with a courageous, withering honesty, admitting, as she does, that history and fantasy congeal when a Black woman loves a white man. He is no longer master. She is no longer a slave. But love does not magically dissolve racist attitudes. Sleeping with a white man doesn't automatically free a Black woman from racial demons of her own.

The first man to ever tell me I was beautiful was white. A photographer. In Tacoma, Washington. I don't remember exactly why he happened to be at my mother's house, but I do remember him saying when we were introduced, "My God, you should be in *Vogue.*" I was seventeen then, bone thin, wearing a batiked mini-dashiki. "Stunning" is the word I believe he used.

Five years later, at a party in Seattle, I was standing around with the other black women that evening feeling very un-stunning. We were watching the brothers present dancing with the white women present. It was a routine occurrence in a town that would later earn the distinction of having the highest incidence of interracial unions of any city in the country. That summer night, however, before time and distance gave me some perspective and success gave me confidence, I took the behavior of the brothers personally, and gave in to the brooding self-hatred typical of so many black women who grow up under the proverbial ugly stick. I was too dark, too tall, too full-featured, too short-haired—too un-white—to be beautiful, to be desired.

So when the lone white boy at the party asked me to dance, I first felt surprise, then a surge of something akin to satisfaction. He was tall, good-looking, a ponytail-wearing hippie cut from the swagger cloth of Johnny Cash. After the dance, a brother—short, pudgy—suddenly appeared at my side. He asked for the next dance. The white man asked for the dance after him. Then the brother. Then "the man." I loved the attention—and the discomfort it caused. The brother was clearly only making a play to make a point to the white man. Serves them right, I thought, looking at the rest of the black men in the room, who had grown implacably sullen, silent. Now they know how the sisters feel.

What I had never thought about until then was how white men might feel. The one pursuing me at the party told me soon enough. "You know, when I first saw you walk through the door tonight, all I wanted to do was fuck you," he said with chilling, cynical honesty. "But now that I see you've got a brain, and I can talk to you, I think I'd like to get to know you."

Of all the ways a white man can get to know a black woman, fucking is clearly the route he has taken most. Sex blazes through the landscape of America's racial history as hot and heavy as the lash of slavery. Sordid, illicit, sinful. Shame branded in skin color. It is our slave past, with its legacy of rape, violation, and miscegenation, that has traditionally defined and colored much of black women's relationships with white men.

Consequently, for the most part, black women do not easily factor white men into the equation of desirables when seeking men to mate and marry. Unlike the white woman for whom the black man has always loomed as stud, an acknowledged sex dream, black women have seldom had such fantasies about white males of the species. There is too much dirty water under the bridge for us to find the white man a likely turn-on.

And yet there have always been black women in the sexual company of white men. We tend to think of them mostly as women who were forced to be whores during slavery, or paid to be whores in freedom, not as cherished, contemporary women who may be respected as girlfriends or revered as wives. The fact of the matter is, there have always been black women and white men who love and want each other.

But desire, especially when mixed with race and sex in America, too often gets mired in fantasy and stereotype, guilt and hypocrisy. We black women endlessly discuss the presumed fascination of black men with white women, but rarely do we talk about that other shoe on the other foot—*our* sexual attraction to white men. True, there are still far greater instances of coupling between the black male and the white female than the other way around, but the numbers of black women who have chosen to join white men in marriage as partners or in bed as lovers has virtually tripled in the last twenty years. The phenomenon is certainly in large measure a response to the black male shortage in our community —a response requiring a certain capacity to ignore history; the grace to absolve the sins of the fathers from succeeding generations of the sons.

The truth is, any time a black woman makes the decision to "go with" a white man, it is usually done consciously, deliberately, sometimes with great shrewdness and always with an understanding of the implications. When I was a senior at the University of Washington, where in 1969 the school's student body of thirty thousand had a black enrollment of about two hundred, a group of four black women friends got together one day and made the practical decision to "start dating white guys." There were too few black men on campus for too many black women, they said. There were too many brothers into white women; too many brothers who were just all-around dogs. So what was a sister to do?

What struck me most about their decision was the swiftness with which they were able to carry it out. Within a month everyone of them was in a steady relationship with a white guy— perfectly respectable white guys, at that, who not only courted the sisters, but genuinely honored them. What finally struck me was the extent to which white men are able see the beauty and value of black women in ways our own men often do not, though these are precisely the same ways in which black men are able to see the beauty and value of white women. Familiarity does perhaps indeed breed contempt for men and women of like race. Opposites do, in fact, probably attract if left unencumbered by the weight of history and stereotype.

I myself was weighed down by both until my mid-twenties. I came to view every white man who made a pass with the same disdain I wound up feeling for the white boy at the party who had so crassly announced that his first instinct when he saw me was to fuck. Wasn't that what all white men really wanted with black women like me?—us Amazon, exotic-savage, bright-and-articulate types, who "have a brain," and thus the power to turn on the two heads white men prize most: the one above the neck and the one below the belt.

What finally got me up off my own prejudices and into the bed of a white man was the oldest aphrodisiac of all—power. We met at another party in another city. This time I had a date—with a black man who worked for the same university I did. The party was being hosted by the university president for a select, elite few. My date informed me at the last minute that he would meet me at the event. He had been asked to accompany some other university officials to the party—people obviously more select and elite than I, was the implicit message.

Angry, I almost didn't go, but then decided not to let one social-climbing black man keep me from pursuing ambitions of my own. The university was threatening to cut off funds for a campus publication I edited, and I needed to make personal appeals to some of the key administrators who would be there. So I arrived alone and on my own.

I had scarcely entered the room before the university's provost, a hulking blond Viking type, zeroed in on me like radar tracking Scuds. "What are you drinking?" he asked with a silly grin. He was already slightly drunk and already seemingly smitten. He spent the rest of the evening following me around like a lovesick puppy dog, occasionally blurting out to anyone within earshot, "Isn't she something?"

When I excused myself to go to the ladies' room, my date (whom I had completely forgotten about) suddenly materialized, buttonholing me in the corridor. His light-skinned face was florid, sweaty, immobilized by rage. "So, I see you're talking to Mr. Provost himself," he hissed. "Well, everybody knows he's into fucking black women."

"Well, sweetheart," I hissed back, "so are you."

The provost, as it turned out, did indeed have a predilection for women of color. Over the course of what was to become a five-year, jagged relationship stuck in angst and conflict (for both of us), I learned of what he called his lunchtime "trysts" with a graduate student from Tanzania, his long and committed friend-ship with a Jamaican woman and her family in Brooklyn, his regular sojourns to Tobago, where his troubled, WASP midwest-ern spirit seemed to find a balm in the heat of the island sun and the arms of island women.

We didn't become sexually intimate for several months, but we quickly became something resembling friends, for we had big fun. We went to Indian restaurants to hear sitar music, to the one Italian restaurant in the city where the waiters sang opera, to after-hours joints for breakfast. He took me to the racetrack on my birthday and staked all my bets; picked up my parents at the air-port when they came for a visit; made clever, witty jokes that cracked me up—like the time he said with a perfectly straight face to the Puerto Rican busboy who was clearing tables at the restau-rant where we were having dinner and had asked him, "You finish?": "Actually, no, I'm Dutch and German."

He was different, not just white and male, but powerful and erudite, privileged and confident—not at all what I was used to. Which, of course, became the turn-on. But like most black women, I first had to overcome my own sexual stereotypes about white men: They couldn't get it on like black men. Didn't have the right stuff. And who wanted to kiss those slits that passed for lips, or stroke that stringy hair? Much to my surprise and dismay, it turned out that I did.

What I remember most about the night we finally made love is that both of us screamed during most of the sex. Not just because we came at the same time (which we did) or because the passion was consuming, explosive, and total (which it was), but because we had reached a place both primal and eternal—and also terri-fying. We had crossed over into the light of pure sexual energy, that primitive mindfield where there is no black or white, no tribal memory, no hurts of history. There is only raw, unrelenting pleasure.

I felt guilty, ashamed, politically incorrect. I was not supposed to experience great sex with a white man. What was wrong with me? Did I really harbor an unconscious desire to be ravished by the oppressor? Was that my particular rape fantasy? My specific slave pathology?

He was no better. He sat up all night after that first time we had sex, drinking whatever liquor he could get his hands on, smoking two packs of cigarettes. Our passion gave us a kind of carnal knowledge that made us uncomfortable, unable to relate in ways that were healthy. He rarely spent the night at my place, nor I at his. Our conversations were always intellectually intense, stimulating, marked by bantering, repartee, stinging one-liners, mind games. But sex framed the dimension of our real discussions; it was only when we made love that we seemed to really "talk," to find natural expression and release, always with a cosmic passion that made us feel our very existence depended on fucking. We continued to go out, but never socialized with any of our friends, and continued to see "other people," more appropriate people, from our own race. I began to feel like the mistress to a repressed white boy, his dirty little secret, and then began to wonder why I thought of myself in such cheap terms.

In the end, our affair sort of withered away, parched in the heat of its own pathology. We never did succeed in getting beyond the stereotypes or letting go of the historical baggage. It was rumored that the reason he had never married—and had a drinking problem—was because he couldn't reconcile the essential truth of his preferences with the expectations of his station. For a fair-haired golden boy, a master of the universe from the cornfields of Iowa, visceral attractions to women like me were considered deviant, emotions that you unleashed in the dark but didn't acknowledge in the light of day.

I sometimes think we might have made it if I had tried a little harder, taken more responsibility, as women usually do, for tending to the feelings in the relationship rather than spending so much time working to prove I was his intellectual equal and not his exotic savage. But I had my own repressions, my own hang-ups (thinking I had to prove my humanity to a white man turned out to be one of them). Like him, in the end I just didn't have the heart, lacked the moral courage, couldn't be free.

It wasn't surprising, then, that the next white man to capture my attention was one free enough to tell me exactly how he felt. "You were obviously the most beautiful woman in the room," he said the first time he called. (Obviously to me, I wasn't, but the fact that he thought I was certainly made an impression.) We had met at a political fund-raiser where we were introduced by a mutual friend. I gave him my number and he called the next day. He was Jewish, though his pale skin, jet-black wavy hair, and rakish mustache made him look, as a friend once told him, like a Latin matinee idol who starred in grade-B movies.

He was a struggling playwright, unemployed because he had quit his nine-to-five yuppie job as an ad salesman "to write." During our third date, which was at his apartment, where he had invited me for dinner, he started off the evening moaning about being out of work. "Oh, please, I have no sympathy," I quickly told him. "You're white and male, and can get a job anytime you want to. You *choose* not to have a job right now, which sure isn't true for most black men who are unemployed. I've known too many who are probably smarter than you and more talented who can't get a break of any kind. So don't whine to me."

My barrage shut him up, but also seemed to turn him on. At one point he glanced up from stirring the spaghetti sauce, gave me a long, appraising look, and finally blurted out, "You know, I'm not into black women. I mean," he quickly went on, "I don't want you to think I'm seeing you because I've got some sexual thing about black women. I don't. The truth is, I've dated a couple of black women before, but I found them to be pathetic. In fact, I find most black people to be pathetic."

It was my turn to shut up. I was dumbstruck by the arrogance, the raw gall—the racism—of this greaseball. "Just what do you mean by that," I finally managed to say, feeling anger start to rise.

"Come on," he said, sounding impatient. "You know what I mean. Everything with them is race. Race this and race that. They don't seem to have any esteem, any sense of themselves beyond being black, black, black."

"*Them?*" I fired back, angry for real. "In case you haven't noticed, sweetheart, I happen to be one of *them*. I happen to be black."

"Oh, but dahling, you're such a prince-seth," he fired back, letting his exaggerated lisp of the word "princess" fall through the air like confetti. Twenty-four years of therapy (he had been going to his shrink since the age of sixteen) had given him, if not great insight or a cure for what ailed him, clearly an opinion on everything and a good degree of humor. I was different, he told me. (Aren't we all?) I didn't use race as an excuse; didn't let it hold me down, keep me from accomplishing things. I seemed to have a powerful sense of myself. I was a whole, healthy person. Right.

Over the next year we did manage to have a fairly whole and healthy relationship. We talked about everything, incessantly. Race, politics, art, his shrink, my career, which at the time was considerably more successful than his, though that never really bothered him. And whenever something really did bother him, he had the hilarious, neurotic habit of simply wailing "Waaaah!" We went to movies and plays, concerts, restaurants, parties with his friends or mine. His unemployment never prevented him from courting me in a style I suppose he thought princesses were accustomed to, something I would always love and admire him for. Sex was good and frequent.

But what intrigued me, kept me excited, was the freedom with which he, like most white men, was able to move through life. He seemed to possess authentic power, a sense of entitlement. He would tell you straight up, "I want to be rich and famous," though as a playwright, Neil Simon he was not. Yet his belief in himself was firm, total. He rose everyday at six, wrote for at least six hours. When he found no producers for his first play, he staged it himself, financing the production with a line of credit from his bank. The run was limited, the reviews mixed, so then he went out and got a job—and started work on his next play. With neither the legacy of slavery nor the current reality of race discrimination to wear him down, he remained buoyed by an optimistic sense of his own possibilities.

We genuinely liked each other with enough respect and passion and sense of fun to feel a kind of comfortable love. Enough so that we occasionally talked about marriage, even said we ought to meet each other's parents, which we finally did.

When he met mine, they were cordial, but less than thrilled. "He's not very tall, is he?" was my mother's first assessment, followed by the ubiquitous "Well, he sure doesn't look Jewish." My father mumbled something about "I guess if he makes you happy . . ."

On the evening I was to meet his parents, he informed me that he had not bothered to mention to them the little detail of my race. "If I told them you were black, it would imply that I think you're different," he said defensively. "Like you were blind, or had polio or something." Besides, he kept reminding me, his parents were old leftist liberals who had been Communists in the forties and regularly had black guests in their home.

This, we were to learn, however, was not the same as discovering who's coming to dinner with your one and only Jewish son. His mother actually passed out when she met me, though she had the social decency to remain upright and keep her eyes open. Her handshake was the giveaway—limp, drained, unconscious. His father kept it together a little better. It wasn't until we got to the restaurant and had ordered drinks that he asked for a cigarette. He had stopped smoking a year ago. The evening quickly went downhill from there, foreshadowing what would be the eventual direction of my relationship with their son.

Race, we had to admit, did matter. In this case, Mommy and Daddy made it clear there would be no inheritance if their only child was seriously entertaining marrying a black woman. They later softened this position and came to accept me, preferring, I suspect, even a black woman in the family to the prospect of a forty-year-old son perhaps never marrying anyone. But it was too late. The son was devastated. The liberal politics of his parents had been a lie, he said, a sham. He was depressed.

I, on the other hand, felt liberated. I knew I could make the move to marriage with this white man if the feeling was mutual, and not be destroyed if it wasn't. It turned out he could not do the same. "Isn't that something?" I said to him the day we parted. "I love you, but can let you go. You can't get past what you think is the betrayal of your parents. I guess that makes me, a black woman, superior to you, a white man. Isn't that something?"

"Waaah!" was all that he could say.

So what can *I* finally say on the subject of interracial love and sex between black women and white men? Would I "do it" again with a white man? If I liked him and he excited me, why not? Do I want to marry out of my race? Have "mixed" children? Not really. Like most black women, I still prefer to make that long, committed haul in the company of a black man. He is my natural partner, the one who affirms me, speaks my language, moves to my rhythm.

And yet I have learned some important lessons—not just about myself, but about men, both black and white—in my specific relationships with white men. The truth, I've now observed first-hand, is that all men are very much the same, regardless of color, or even personal circumstance. They all have an equal capacity to be smart and funny, stupid and crazy, insecure, cool, jive, honor-able, demanding, and troubled; as well as tender and loving and thrilling between the sheets.

What's different, and significant, is how black men and white men perceive their reality and their power, both of which define the nature of their relationships to women. Black nationalist Haki Madhubuti contends that black men and white men are virtually engaged in a state of war, which may explain why so many in our community consider black women who sleep with white men to

be sleeping with the enemy. But the truth, I've found, is that race
and sex are never quite so black and white. The enemy is often
within, and the war between black men and white men is usually
over what war tends to always be about: power and control, ego
and honor, profits and privilege—not about us women neces-
sarily, but about men being men.

Black Men, White Women:

A Sister Relinquishes Her Anger

BEBE
MOORE CAMPBELL

Bebe Moore
Campbell fesses up and releases a long-held anger at Black men involved
with white women, a bitterness stoked over most of her adult life. Remembering the swaggering boldness with which many of the "bruthahs," freed
by the civil rights movement and the cataclysms of Black Power, laid claim
to white women, Campbell captures the awful "twixt-and-tweenness"
Black women felt then and often feel still, watching Black men "talk
Black and sleep white." But at the intersection of personal freedom and
loyalty to the race, the choices, Campbell concedes, are private, not in the
public domain.

$\mathbf{T}$here is a story that has been wending its way through the cocktail–and–house party circuit of middle-class African-American communities in large urban cities. Two wealthy black businessmen are strolling down the street and one says to the other, "Man, let's try to get a date with the next white women we see." His friend agrees and soon they notice two white women approaching them. One is young and pretty; the other is over seventy, not very attractive, and has difficulty walking. One of the men says quickly, "I want the old one." His amazed companion asks, "Why in the world do you prefer her?"

"Because she's been white longer."

In some circles "The White Girl Joke" is met with stony silence, considered not so much humorous as it is a searing social commentary that strikes far too close to home to evoke laughter. For many African-American women, the thought of black men, particularly those who are successful, dating or marrying white women is like being passed over for the prom by the boy of their dreams, causing them pain, rage, and an overwhelming sense of betrayal and personal rejection.

According to the U.S. Census Bureau, in 1970 there were 41,000 couples where the husband was black and the wife white, and by 1988 there were 149,000. The national totals for black women married to white men have increased also, from 24,000 in 1970 to 69,000 in 1988. Only 3.6 percent of black men are married to women who aren't black. But if the amount doesn't seem significant enough to warrant an outcry from black women, it's because numbers alone don't tell the whole story. A new African-American proverb says it best: In a drought, even one drop of water is missed.

African-American women are thirsty for black men, whose ranks have been decimated by homicides, incarceration, and drug addiction in greater proportions than other groups. At the same time that interracial marriages have increased, marriages for African-American women have decreased: 48 percent of all black women of marriageable age are either divorced or have never married, compared to 31 percent of white women. And when black men and women do come together, for a host of reasons, not the least of which is the likelihood that their incomes are significantly lower than those of whites, they are more likely to divorce than any other group. But if alliances with black men are a battlefield strewn with land mines, most black women say they prefer a war zone to loneliness. Some, particularly single ones, respond with anger and hostility to what they perceive to be raids by white female troops, asserting that white women are succumbing to the highly sexualized image of the African-American male as phallic symbol. If there are other reasons they are with black men—true love, for example—black women don't want to hear about them. Their anger only partially conceals dual core issues: the humiliation of being rejected for not measuring up to an image of femininity that excludes them, and the underlying paranoia that one day all their men may be taken captive by the enemy and they will have no one.

"In our society to be white is to be privileged," explains Professor Reginald Daniel, who teaches multiethnic identity at the University of California in Los Angeles. "To be a white female is to rank at the top of beauty standards. A person without that background has to work hard to feel okay." African-American women's egos are still bleeding from years of white society's oppression and denigration of their dark, full-featured beauty and more independent brand of womanhood. Many "sisters" grew up taking solace in the notion that they had a God-given, inalienable right to expect that the "brothers" on the planet were reserved for them—and vice versa, that their men loved and valued them above all other women. But integration has led to multifaceted interaction between the races and an end to the kind of sexual apartheid that used to keep blacks and whites apart. Some African-American females say that they feel psychologically assaulted when they perceive that black men favor and idealize white women simply because of their color. They believe that they are being penalized, not only because of the way they look, but because they possess the emotional strength that, while essential during the eras of slavery and segregation, isn't deemed quite feminine enough for today's black man on the rise.

"Black men are brainwashed to adore white skin," says Dolores Williams, founder and president of Black Women's Alliance, a support group. "They malign us to nonblacks to justify their own behavior. The black man will do more for a white woman than the white man will. He'll work two or three jobs to put a white girl through school. Of course white women chase them. They know they're an easy touch."

Others declare that black men seek to align themselves with white women because they believe they are more willing to be subservient than black women. "The common stereotype is that white women, particularly college-age ones, will do anything for a black man," says Gayle Pollard Terry, who is black. "African-American women make much greater demands on men. I think that basically a lot of black men see white women as trophies."

"There is jungle fever," admits Michael Hughes, forty, who has lived with a white woman for more than fifteen years, "and black men and white women are more prone to being fascinated just because of skin color." Hughes asserts that his own choice of a lover has less to do with being turned on by white skin and is more about finding a cultural comfort zone. "I'm an odd person; I don't dance," he says. "Black people always transmitted to me this presumption of who I was as though that was finite. It's easier for the odd black man not to deal with race expectations and to be with white folks." Other black men declare that black women are too materialistic, too argumentative, too demanding. Just too much.

Regardless of the statement black men with white women want to make, or even if they wish to make one, what many black women receive is a hurtful mixture of blatant sexism and eerie internecine racism: If you were good enough (if you looked like white women and didn't give me so much back talk), I wouldn't choose someone else. The message that they don't measure up makes some sisters want to scream.

I know the feeling.

Days after I first heard The White Girl Joke, some friends and I —all African-American women—were sitting in a trendy Beverly Hills restaurant having lunch when a good-looking, popular black actor strolled in. As an audible buzz of recognition traveled from table to table, my friends and I—restrained star-gazers all—managed to surreptitiously turn our heads toward the handsome celebrity without sacrificing one iota of our collective cool. That is, until we saw the blonde trailing behind him.

Our synchronized forks hit the plates on the first beat. An invisible choir director only we could see raised her hands: All together now. In unison, we moaned, we groaned, we rolled our eyes heavenward. We gnashed our teeth in harmony and made ugly faces. We sang "Umph! Umph! Umph!" a cappella–style, then shook our heads as we lamented for the ten thousandth time the perfidy of black men and cursed trespassing white women who dared to "take our men." The fact that I am married to my second black husband didn't lessen the fervor of my rendition of this same old song one bit. Had Spike Lee ventured in with a camera and recorder, he would have had the footage and sound-track for *Jungle Fever Part II, III,* and *IV.* Before lunch was over I had a headache, indigestion, and probably elevated blood pressure. In retrospect, I think I may have shortened my life considerably. To add insult to injury, my last glimpse of the blonde and the brother revealed that they were so intent on gazing into each other's eyes that they were oblivious to our stellar performance.

As I drove home with my head pounding and my heart racing, I slowly came to a conclusion that I'd been avoiding for a long time: in the multiracial society that Americans live in, to feel that one has exclusive rights to the members of the opposite sex of one's race is a one-way ticket to Migraine City. I don't want to live there anymore. It is time for me to relinquish the wrath I feel toward black men and white women and move on.

Let me be clear: I'm not ashamed of my fury. The resentment and even hostility that I harbor are perfectly normal, and I believe that my sisters and I have conducted ourselves with ladylike dignity and enormous restraint. We're not slashing brothers' tires; we're not cutting off white girls' hair. We're just obsessing; anyone in our situation would do the same. "All races and even some ethnic and religious groups have a sense of proprietary rights over the opposite sex members of their society," says Belinda Tucker, Ph.D., who with a partner, Claudia Mitchell-Kernan, Ph.D., has conducted a study at UCLA of interracial dating patterns among African Americans. "These feelings are a form of social control." Immigrants from Ireland, Italy, Poland, and other countries experienced bitterness several generations ago in America when the first of their European clan began "marrying out." "Other people besides black women absolutely feel resentment," says Dr. Tucker. "It is difficult for anyone who identifies with just one group to see interracial dating and marriage and not worry."

In California, where most Asians reside, in some ethnic groups more than 80 percent marry out—more than any other people— to partners who are most likely white. Although some Asian women accuse their men of abandoning them for big-breasted, blue-eyed blondes, in direct contrast to African Americans, these Asian/white marriages are four times as likely to be between white men and Asian women. In a society where tall, muscular hunks are viewed as the ideal, Asian men say that their image has been neutered and they are angry about being abandoned. Antonio De Castro, forty, a Filipino photographer, says that lots of Asian men sit around and gripe about the trend. "They say, 'Why are all the fine Asian women going out with white guys?' There are Asian women who consciously choose not to date men like themselves because they believe being with white men elevates their social status or because they feel their biracial children will be more beautiful than Asian kids. You ask all of them why they're with white men and they'll say they just happened to fall in love. But something else is going on besides true love. It's an issue of self-contempt," says De Castro, who in the last two years has tried to woo back Asian women by publishing a beefcake calendar of well-muscled, scantily clad Asian men.

Asian women respond to accusations that they are abandoning their race by saying that their brothers are sexist and that white males don't put restraints on them. Some white women tend to view the phenomenon with resentment and suspicion, believing that they are being discarded because white men are attracted by the notion of subservient China dolls and geisha girls, preferring them to "feminist" Caucasians. There are white women who also react jealously when they see white males with African-American women.

In the Jewish community, where more than half of all marriages are interfaith, Orthodox and Conservative rabbis refuse to marry "mixed" couples. Some Jewish women believe that "their" men are programmed to prefer the "shiksa," or Gentile woman. "Many Jewish women will never have blond hair, narrow hips, and slender thighs," explains Robin Warshaw, forty-two, the author of *I Never Called It Rape,* who is married to a Christian. "When they see Jewish men who've chosen women like that, who dismiss them as nagging and materialistic Jewish-American Princesses, it stirs up resentment. You feel betrayed."

Bri Franchot, thirty-two, a casting director who grew up Christian, has long dark blond hair that has attracted Jewish men and the ire of some of those women. "I was at a party surrounded by Jewish women who were complaining that they couldn't find men of their religion to date, and I said it seemed as though that's all I met," says Franchot. "One of the women turned to me and said, 'You're what they want to date. You're the Shiksa Goddess.' I think there was some resentment in that remark."

"I go to conferences where there are intellectual Latino men, and they are all with white women," says Sandra Cisneros, thirty-seven, the author of *Woman Hollering Creek*. She declares that when Henry Cisneros (no relation), the former mayor of San Antonio, admitted to having an affair with a blonde, Mexican-American, women in the city were furious. She says, "Latina women always talk about brown men and white women among ourselves. Our rage is real and so is our pain. I think Latino men don't love us the way we love them."

African-American men, who according to Dr. Tucker's study are the most likely to date outside their race, aren't immune to expressing resentment when they see "their" women dating other men. On a recent "Arsenio Hall Show," black actress Rae Dawn Chong told the audience how the black owner of a barbecue restaurant ordered her and her white ex-husband out of his restaurant because he disapproved of the interracial couple. Throughout the history of this country, white males have reacted violently to even the implication that white women might consort with outsiders. "I am much more afraid of white male hostility than that of black women," says Jean Bernard, Michael Hughes's white lover. "I still think of white males as capable of violence."

But if my anger is within the range of predictable and acceptable group norms, it is increasingly uncomfortable for me personally, like a horrrifying LSD trip I can't escape. Anger has become a habit, an addiction. And as with any quick high, I can get a fix almost anywhere. There are, of course, black women who couldn't care less about whom any man besides their man is with. And according to Dr. Tucker, black women are more likely to date outside their race than women of other groups. Still, almost every time I get together with two or more African-American women, the topic turns to "the problem." We're disgusted; we're fascinated. We're obsessing; we're PMSing. We operate on a blatant double standard, thrilling to tabloid gossip that Robert De

Niro is "into sisters," but castigating black male celebrities who have deserted us. I'm tired of putting my mood at the mercy of chance encounters with strangers. I'm too old for this shit.

I want peace of mind. I am ready to relinquish my anger.

Yes, I want my people to date and marry each other and I don't think it will ever give me pleasure to see black men with white women, but my wanting it isn't going to make it happen. My being angry isn't going to make white women and black men stop choosing each other. The only thing I can control regarding this phenomenon is my response to it. My goal isn't to enjoy the fact that some black men prefer white women to the women of their own race. I'm simply trying to live with it, as sanely as I can. What I'm striving for is the same feeling I get whenever I run into my ex-husband: neutrality. I can acknowledge the man without giving up any energy or emotions. I worked for years to achieve that kind of peace of mind; it is a wonderful blessing.

I guess I'll have to retrain my mind, learn to take deep breaths when I see black men and white women, maybe even smile. Meditation might help and I'll try it, if I can sit still long enough. I suppose that what I must do is forgive those black men who've hurt me. All the New Age, spiritual books I read recommend this. They say forgiveness cleanses the spirit. I certainly want my spirit cleansed.

What is even more pressing than having a clean spirit, though, is passing on the right message to my fifteen-year-old daughter, Maia, who now finds herself contending with the same issues that have caused her mother and other older black women so much pain. Not long ago Maia went to a party. Her mood had been happy when she left, but when I picked her up, she was silent and gloomy. I asked the usual motherly questions. Was the party fun? Grunt. Did she have a good time? Grunt. Did she dance? Grunt. I was about to give up when she said suddenly, her tone venomous, "The black boys only asked the white girls to dance."

Looking at my child's crestfallen face, I contemplated all the things, both practical and soothing, that I could say to her. I thought about the legacies I wanted to pass on to her and the ones I didn't. I thought about the kind of woman I wanted her to be and the kind I didn't want her to become. And then I thought about my own childhood and a special woman who permeated it.

As a child, I remember sitting in my bedroom in the dark with a hair clip on my nose, trying to reduce the size of my wide nostrils. Later, when the teenage parties I attended grew hot and my hair turned "nappy," I would dash into the bathroom and attempt to repair the damage with a frail comb not up to the task, so the boys wouldn't see how ugly I was. While I was growing up I recall watching my grandmother make pancakes and seeing Aunt Jemima's face on the box. Aunt Jemima has a new, modern hairdo now, but she is still on the pancake box, a sturdy, sensible woman, not unpleasant to look at, but clearly one who is meant for servitude and not adoration. And what I knew then, I know now: when some people look at me, or any black woman, they see Aunt Jemima: a mammy, built to serve, not to adore. A few of those people are *my* men.

I can't change anyone's perception of me; I can only love myself better, hold all the facets of me in high esteem. The thing I like about Sister Jemima is this: she's a survivor.

I don't want my child or me held hostage by our own rage. I want us to endure through the decades, smiling and knowing that no one can reject us unless we give them permission to do so. So, what I finally said to Maia was this: "Don't get angry about it, honey. That's the worst thing you can do. People have the right to be with whomever they choose. Those choices don't have anything to do with you personally, unless you think they do."

In the land where Marilyn Monroe's beauty still reigns supreme, few black women emerge unscathed . . . and few black men. Some brothers may need to ask themselves why they are with white women, particularly those who use them as emotional props to soothe wounded psyches and maybe even those who are truly in love; it isn't my responsibility to conduct the interrogation. If like me, my brothers need to embark upon the path that leads to the resurrection of their damaged souls, then I urge them to read the books, attend the seminars, or choose the therapist and begin their journey.

I forgive black men for hurting me: I forgive me for letting them.

I am moving toward peace.

Mars

Conjunct Neptune

JUDY
DOTHARD SIMMONS

Nurturing and loving the self unadorned, unchanged by marriage. Respecting and asserting the validity of singleness. Changing its connotation from minus, incomplete, to a complex, full-blown existence guided by its own possibilities. This is one of the most dramatic challenges inherent in contemporary feminism.

Judy Dothard Simmons wrestles with the often contradictory process of accepting the promise of what has been called "single blessedness." There have always been women willing to go it alone. Today more of us are able to articulate why remaining single is not second-class citizenship but a first-class way of life.

The love relationships I've had strike me now as recurring episodes of a chronic illness—one that I suffered for forty-odd years before a cure was discovered. Or, as serving hard time for the crime of wanting to have sex and other adventures with men, but not wanting to stay with one forever.

My last lover flung the charge at me, "You don't have the courage to have a man or a child." Part of me got properly upset, as girls are supposed to when accused of being frigid, lesbian, bitchy, selfish, or otherwise independent of the men they love.

But the part of my computer that he didn't have the password for sniggered at both of us playacting fools: "Do you think I'm stupid? I wouldn't trap myself like that, especially not for love."

I figure my last-gasp, turning-forty fling with him was one of the "I was sick at the time" affairs. Instead of making the most of the hard-earned graduate fellowship I had for the 1984–85 term at Columbia University, I opted to be his faithful partner—and to make his needs, responsibilities, and goals my own. I decided to support him economically as well as emotionally while he made the transition from being a fallen numbers king (and practitioner of God knows what other thuggery) to being an upstanding technician.

He really needed the help, since he and his recently acquired third wife produced two children less than eighteen months apart, and he had to feed the alcohol and cocaine habits that I didn't even know about for some considerable time.

For my part, I needed a personal life. I'd been pouring myself out over the airwaves of New York for several years, operating what amounted to a psychological counseling service and a school-without-walls on the radio, and I was drained. I wanted some shelter.

Naturally I started out enchanted. He came into my life still:

> *sheathed in the primal*
> *radiance of creation over*
> *golden dust of flesh and*
> *glittering ashes from karmic returns*

'Course those lines were inspired by a brief encounter with another guy five or six years earlier, but that's how they look to me —the men who move me enough to ease past my Virgo finickiness and leave fingerprints on my private parts. Like Saul/Paul on the road to Damascus, I'm struck by a blinding brightness that calls me to my Lord of Love. I just can't effing see.

Make no mistake about it, having sex, making love, fucking—by whatever name, when I'm moved to meld with a man, it's a metaphysical experience. In recent years, and in some circles, the idea has grown that sex can be addictive, like alcohol and cocaine. I guess that means it creates an altered state. Well, it does for me, but not like a weekend drug escapade.

With physical sex as the vehicle, I enter the realm of the psychic and spiritual. I see my own psyche as if it were an aerial view of a landscape. I travel to regions of old hurt, peaks of good feeling, and huge lakes of longing that shrink, during the act, to dewdrops pooling on a leaf.

And I become attuned to the man. One time around 1976 I was in bed with a friend who didn't attract me physically. I had a lot of respect for his struggle with life, though; and I was grateful for his admiration, encouragement, and, yes, love of me as I made my shaky way in New York City. He was also a man in great need of physical healing. He'd been at death's door several times from various cardiovascular incidents.

We were lying face-to-face, naked, with our legs entangled but our torsos separated by six inches or so. No way did I want to fuck this guy, but I sure wanted to give him something as vital to him as his caring was to me, and, typically, he thought fucking me was what he needed. So I prepared myself by concentrating on the one desire I did have for him—to see him whole, healthy, and happy.

Somehow my own wants and preferences moved aside and I began to feel a pulsing warmth. After some moments, I glanced down between our bodies and saw a two-inch-wide bar of yellowish orange light extend out of my solar plexus and touch his side. The bar steadied and remained between us, rippling as something—energy, for lack of a better word—flowed in through the top of my head and out through my middle into his body.

He felt something, a warmth he told me later, and looked down also. We remained still for a time, nanoseconds, minutes, I don't know. Then he jerked back suddenly, breaking the connection, and proceeded to scramble up on top of me as if to commence the usual and far inferior form of uniting. I tried to go with it for a minute, but my heart wasn't in it. I was bitterly disappointed. He had refused a miracle so he could act the stud.

He said as much to me after I'd made him cease and desist. He told me he'd seen the light, literally, and felt the energy. He said he even realized that a healing process had begun, but he got scared. He couldn't be that passive, was how he put it; he couldn't allow himself to be entered, even metaphysically. He had to be in the saddle. His manhood depended on it.

Clearly we were out of phase, as I usually have been with men. The gap between the relationships I envision and those I actually have has been too wide for me to span with a commitment. That would be like shopping for high-heeled, sling-back sandals and ending up with Army boots. I yearned for what I now know is an inhuman, impossible magic. I didn't want a man for domestic and family life. I wanted him to give me the ultimate aesthetic experience. *If you want to be loved by a poet,* I once wrote, *you must be her endless and ultimate poem.*

My last lover rightly sensed there was a truth I was ducking, but it wasn't that I feared to marry and reproduce. I was scared to acknowledge that I'd decided not to. I didn't want to tie myself down with children, work like a dog outside the home and in, and just generally be an SBW, Strong Black Woman—which has long translated to me as a BOB, Beast of Burden.

Given the tremendous social pressure to carry that old rugged cross, I think it takes a lot of guts not to just lie down at some point and give up on your deepest dream. But you pay for whatever you do, whether it's what you want or what "they" say you ought to do. So, you might as well pay for pleasing yourself. My Mom has big trouble with that idea. Her life convinced her that the very last thing you do is what you want to do.

I look at what she's put in for what she's reaped and feel she's been shortchanged, at least from the viewpoint of my Capricorn Moon in the Second House.★ To give up as much of herself as she has to the stony ground of two self-centered husbands, several stepchildren, and me, even, is, in my view, to have missed the point of being here on the planet. Mom has been hardworking, faithful, loyal, and self-sacrificing. And loving.

And loving is hard on you:

> . . . hold me, trace
> stretch marks striating
> my breasts and the
> butcher's scar stitching
> my abdomen as if the

★ In astrology, the moon represents a person's emotional nature. The sign it's in shows how the emotional nature expresses itself, and the house it's in shows what areas and affairs of life are most affected by the person's emotions. Some people might say that a woman with a Moon in Capricorn in the Second House is a cold-hearted, gold-digging bitch.

A kinder interpretation is that (a) she doesn't feel that love conquers poverty; (b) her socioeconomic status fluctuates according to her emotional state—and vice versa; and (c) to her, emotional energy is investment capital that has to pay off in tangible ways. She's not likely to be comfortable for long giving more than she gets.

babies came hard and I
gave them too much of
my sustenance/it's one way love uses you . . .

The thing that beats all is that Momma reflects on herself and her life and finds them wanting. Such is the brainwashing laid on women that Momma judges her worth only in terms of marriage and motherhood, despite the fact that she taught and administered schools for more than thirty years.

She was dedicated. Hundreds of people in the horrid little country towns of the South transcended their circumstances because this insightful, extraordinarily loving person cultivated them. Yet, she's a failure in her own eyes because her first husband, my father, divorced her; her second husband ran around on her; and I, her daughter, refuse to go to church, marry before having sex, or enter a respectable profession like teaching.

Never mind that you can't make silk purses out of sows' ears: my eighty-year-old father recently got his sixth divorce, and my late stepfather, well, let's say his agenda didn't include my mother's well-being. And as for the daughter, she's led an interesting life, using all the skills her mother sacrificed to give her: music lessons at four, a typewriter at seven, boarding school at twelve, a taste for adventure, and a sort of canny sight that has kept her out of the worst of jams. What more can any mother wish to accomplish than to raise a kid that stands on its own two feet?

My insides knot and twist and run as I contemplate Momma's life, her sisters', her mother's. While I was growing up, my inescapable love of them tangled into a cat's cradle with my compassion for their swim against the riptide of Negro women's lives, and with my anguished fear that I might get trapped by that same undertow.

At sixteen I told my mother that I would marry a white man if I loved him. She started praying, although that might have been more about my having taken up smoking—I was a freshman in college—than about my willingness to defect to the other side.

When I was eighteen I surrendered my virginity to a French-

Canadian professor at my college, under the impression that we would shortly be married. Since he was Catholic and I a D. H. Lawrence–type Romantic, we didn't use birth control for this single, fumbling, pretty much passionless penetration at a friend's house in Oakland, California.

Ten weeks later I was older and one five-hundred-dollar Mexican abortion wiser. I was only the third woman the guy had touched in his thirty-one years. An ex-seminarian, he was also gay. Clearly my first try at escaping a Negro female fate, by marrying a professional white man, was a fiasco.

At least I had sense enough not to compound the error by starting a child off with only one broke, half-educated teenage parent. Shoot, my mother had been married and had a college degree, but she still had to scrub Jewish women's floors in New York in the fifties (the phone company said she was overqualified; the board of ed discounted her B.S. degree from Johnson C. Smith University); then in Cherokee County, Alabama, where she was finally allowed to work as an educator, she picked cotton to supplement the unequal pittance paid to Negro teachers in the segregated system.

I didn't want to subject a child of mine to my childhood. Mom and I bounced around and were separated a lot when I was a kid, what with trying to get our bearings after the divorce. I had lived in Westerly, Rhode Island; New London and Willimantic, Connecticut; Bronx, New York; and in Choccolocco, Anniston, and Cedar Bluff, Alabama, by the time I was, what, eight?—and never in a house or apartment that I could call "mine."

Living on sufferance is hard on a kid. You can't assert yourself, 'cause it's always somebody else's ball. Sometimes Mom and I were together; sometimes I alone lived with the paternal grandmother, the maternal aunt. Often I was alone when we were together, like the year we lived in a rooming house in Willimantic while we awaited the final divorce decree.

I was the only child there. Mom worked swing shift in a knitting mill. I spent evenings by myself playing Patti Page's recording of "The Tennessee Waltz," very softly, of course, over and over, before putting myself to bed. I was six, but my loneliness and resignation were ageless. As the poet Ai wrote, *the poor don't have children, just small people.*

The next year we were in the Bronx at Mom's father's apartment. He had done quite well, for a Negro, as a Pullman porter over the years, but Mom was nonetheless paying him rent out of the money she earned scrubbing floors on her knees. Need I say that Momma was depressed? Need I say further that Grandpa's stinginess, coupled with my father's desertion, didn't do a lot for my estimation of men?

Ultimately Momma went home to her mother, the benevolent *Generalissima,* who had reared her own three daughters, thirteen children of her second husband, and her brother's four, while also founding and teaching school, working in her husband's general store, and being a pillar of the church.

I went, too, naturally, into the segregated and rural South. I thought I'd descended into hell—unpaved roads, wooden outhouses, no home telephones, well water, burning garbage in a barrel in the yard, finding out that ham and bacon and drumsticks were really pigs and chickens that lived and breathed, grunted, strutted, clucked, shat, gave birth, and had awareness and intelligence. How could anyone bring herself to kill and then *eat* them?

It was all too barbaric. This was what happened to you when you married somebody, had his baby, and then he left. The child was a responsibility, a burden that you carried sacrificially. That might mean lugging your baggage back to rural Alabama after you had managed a nearly miraculous escape in the first place, and picking cotton to feed your kid, and living in rustic cottages, and peeing and shitting in a slop jar, a white enamel pail with a red-bordered lid, into which you poured Clorox to kill bacteria and odor—as if chlorined urine and feces could be less disgusting than *L'Arome de la Merde au Naturel.*

It was what happened to you if you were colored, and married, and had a child, and then he left. You fell down into a hole so deep you could see stars in the daytime. And white folk kept on pushing you down farther and farther, just 'cause they felt like it, and you had no goddamned control of anything, so you had to make your child drink from the COLORED water fountains, sit in the COLORED waiting rooms, stand outside like a beggar to buy a sandwich at the back door of a café, pass the brick white schools with indoor plumbing to get to wooden black schools with the falling-down outdoor toilets that the boys peeked through the cracks between the boards of to see you do your business. I used to go from seven in the morning, when Momma and I left home, to four or five in the afternoon, when we got back, without relieving myself.

So, given that history, when I'm a college junior pregnant out of wedlock, eighteen and broke and on my own in California in 1963, and the guy turns out screwy, do you think I'd take a chance on having a baby when it meant that I, like my mom before me, could end up going home to Mother in Alabama and living that horror all over again? Some slave women aborted their pregnancies and killed their infants rather than have them warped by slavery. I can empathize:

> *hated those country roads*
> *and the sullen smudge of fear on every horizon*
> *Every Black was under casual death threat . . .*

> *We kept a vigil on white people*
> *like a navigator on the Pole Star . . .*

> *Some of us are servile, some wisely humble. Fear and shame*
> *accompany our rage. Granted the dignity of man and all,*
> *we know how much won't kill you. That may, in the end,*
> *kill some of us: wishing we had fought harder and died sooner.*
> *It is a shame to be Black and still alive . . .*

The funny part, of course, is that my childhood in the South in the fifties was better than Momma's had been in the twenties; but I had started out in New England and New York, not on a farm in Choccolocco, Alabama, so the South suffered greatly by comparison. Besides, segregation and racism simply made me crazy from the time I got there at age seven.

The inequalities enraged me; the unfairness of it all ate away at my sense of self, and fostered both envy of and disgust for white culture. On one hand, I grew determined to show "them" I was a refined Negro and a superior person, and to claim what someone of my smarts and sensibilities deserved of the good life in Jane Austen novels. On the other, I came to despise the moral deadness, hypocrisy, and willful ignorance that dominate white American society.

I brought this conflict to what were probably my best possibilities for marriage—the intimate friendships I had with two white men when I was at peak marriage age, twenty-three through twenty-five. I met these good guys, call them Adam and Trenton, when I was teaching in a Job Corps center in 1967, and was Adam's girl while we were all there. Then a year and change later, after the center closed, I broke up with Adam so that Trenton and I could hook up in New York; we became steadies for a year or so.

These were the pleasantest, most well-rounded relationships I've had with men. I still say that, even with twenty-twenty hindsight. We were intellectually compatible, number one, which is not something I've ever shared with my semi-long-term black lovers. The white guys had broad interests, resources, and access: a ski lodge in Twin Mountain, New Hampshire; a 17-foot Corinthian sailboat docked at Mattapoisett, Massachusetts, on Buzzards Bay; penchants for Greek restaurants in Boston and Appalachian Trail hiking through Bear Mountain State Park in New York; memberships in the New York Choral Society and the Museum of Modern Art.

Trent and I played chess, and he hated losing to me. He also worried that I loved his trust fund more than his compulsive Quaker personality. Adam and I loved to fry potatoes with bell peppers and onions, and I gained weight. I went canoeing with Trent and overturned into the Egg Harbor River on the New Jersey–Maryland border (if there is such a contiguity—in the immortal cadence of Carmen McRae, *I, [beat, beat] did-n't know what time it was* back then, much less where we were doing the location shoots for this movie).

I visited Trent's family home in Philadelphia over a Memorial Day weekend, and tiptoed downstairs very early in the morning to make the acquaintance of the black maid—I needed to strike some kind of bargain before I was waited on in a white household by an African-American woman who could have been my mother. (The woman, Blanche, was cool.)

I proved my gentility by playing Ravel's *Pavane pour une infante défunte* on their grand piano, and speaking my usual flawless English, and being just oh-so-impeccably intellectual, and wearing delicate sandals and a dress for a rough walk through adjacent Fairmount Park, when sneakers and shorts were called for, and tripping over a root or rock or something and falling flat on my self-conscious, mortified face.

Adam and Trent didn't think their manhood depended on having two, three, or four women, or on going out with the boys just 'cause being with a bitch alla time ain' cool. They didn't criticize me for not having a Hottentot behind nor expect me to do the watusi. They didn't act as if a suggestion from me about how to fix something was a knife slicing off their balls.

In other words, we didn't touch off each other's insanity, whereas for me, at least, intimate dealings with black men have been trips to the ozone and walks on the wack side. 'Course, as one man pointed out to me, I wasn't going with your average white boy—one of my friends was a Yale graduate and the other had an MBA from Stanford, when MBAs were still the patrimony of a small, moneyed class of WASPs.

By contrast, I was very democratic about my black consorts: though they had to be clean, well-spoken, and natively intelligent, I didn't require that they be educated, well-to-do, cultured, and otherwise socially advantaged. I'd never have gone with a blue-collar white guy. As a group they don't have too much use for black folk, plus, in terms of intellect and values, we generally lack a common language.

I wasn't nearly so dismissive of black men, however. In a way, I was like the liberal white girls who took up with the most Bigger-ish of Negroes in the sixties: I couldn't expect men so socially oppressed to meet the same standards as men advantaged by white-skin privilege.

Now I know I'm not the sort of woman who can live with close relationships that I perceive as unequal; but then I was just finding out who I was and what was possible. Besides, marrying down, as it's inelegantly put, was a Negro tradition, since girls were educated to save them from Miss Anne's kitchen, which too often came equipped with Mr. Charlie's bed.

I never had a black boyfriend of the Ivy League ilk, but that wasn't my doing:

> black Ivy League would marry white
> or, failing that, a yellow bourgeoisie
> and white boys, the professionals,
> don't marry black . . .

That's what I'd observed and experienced by the time I was twenty-five. So at ground level—despite the genuine affection between us—I figured me and these white guys were just going through some motions, before bowing to the inevitable. (Re-member, I'd already struck out once.) Strangely enough, I think I sold both those young men short.

Be that as it may, I rather precipitously ended each of the relationships. Following the partings, both men went through about a year of private and apparently profound attitude adjust-ment, and then seemed to want serious return engagements.

Hey, but I was in the wind by then, and my vagabond life offered no precedent for going back. Being with Adam and Tren-ton was for me like escaping into a movie or a novel, knowing all the while that I had to return to my harsh Negro reality. My loyalties demanded that, and my pride.

Besides, there was too much unexplored history between us,

and we never talked about the role of race in our lives. How could I ever have told them about the slop jar?

Beyond all that, I just felt like I had to go. It always gets to be like that with me, but I didn't call it correctly until I hit my forties: close relationships get on my nerves. I get claustrophobia. I get bored. After a while, my warm, appreciative feelings for the person turn cold, and I just want to be free of having to consider others in my personal space.

Maybe it results in part from the boarding school thing: being regulated and surveilled from twelve to almost sixteen, confined in jail-cell-sized rooms with other girls, after being a country only-child who biked, hiked through woods, read, wrote poems, played piano, and sang in the timeless solitude of the dream life she created to escape the mortal asthma of the truly stultifying South.

I don't need a domestic "other," unless he can be a fellow artist who desires the ultimate collaboration. That's the marriage I dreamed of: a wedding of sensibilities, a union of visions, the yoking of crafts, the birthing of art. It's very Tenth House Mars conjunct Neptune in Libra: partnerships in which sex, spirituality, art, ideals, work, career, and love are all tied up together.

In a way that seems like dreaming, my sense of myself arises from the undifferentiated current that contains all of us, all of everything. The current flows underneath my conscious mind like sleep flows beneath a dream.

I usually feel as though I'm moving through states and out-comes that I visualize only occasionally, and blurrily, as through a glass darkly. I'm a dream-in-progress, then. It has been pretty much beyond me to imagine permanent attachments and lifelong commitments, imbued as I am with perpetual ontological restlessness.

Also, during my twenties, which are typically the marrying years, I was awakening artistically—writing poetry seriously, studying music and piano technique with Roland Hanna, and taking *bel canto* voice lessons from a certifiable depressive with neurotic Siamese cats and a twilight apartment.

I was in a furious state of becoming. Finally I'd alighted in an environment that gave me scope for whatever of myself I could bring into play. I was in the Big Apple, pioneering in corporate management, establishing a presence in the artistic community, and pursuing a confused involvement with a major jazzman, who catalyzed my artistic development.

I wrote. I sang. I played. I worked. I cried. I fucked. I fell apart. I studied astrology, went to shrinkage; got raped; cut my wrists; timed out in Jamaica; tore my telephone out of the wall three or four times in one week because nothing I heard on it made me feel whole and human.

By the time I turned thirty, I'd reached what would be diagnosed in a Western intellectual man as an existential crisis. The things I had believed in, had hoped and striven for up to that point, seemed gossamer indeed when put up against the huge, impersonal evil in the world.

My childhood had shown me that love, marriage, and motherhood didn't guarantee you anything—not companionship, not security, certainly not happiness. My young adulthood showed me that my being smart, hardworking, spiritual, and purehearted didn't exempt me from any of the insults to which my biosocial status entitled me: a person who is female, black, and working-class will be injured by sexism, racism, classism no matter what she does.

However, I was the dream-in-progress, remember? I'd put everything I had into getting out of Alabama, and then done everything from nannying to telephone sales to civil service clerking for seven years to put myself through the hostile white college. I had worked the seventeen-hour days that got me a plum move to company headquarters in New York City, so that I could live in fabled Greenwich Village in middle-class comfort, and have the financial wherewithal to exploit the Apple's resources for my own development.

Then six years in the corporation and four in the city showed me—as it had shown my mother—that there is no escape from Alabama for a black woman in America, not through love, education, career, or art. I sickened from the hatred that drips like acid onto a woman and a black person who kicks against the cage of caste and class. Bitterness, despair, the ashes of defeat leached the color from my world. Shrouded in chill-gray hopelessness, I crawled out of the city and went to ground in Mount Vernon like the wounded animal I was.

For the first time since I'd gone on my own at seventeen, I lived in a black neighborhood. I was on welfare for a while, then Social Security disability. Pioneering for the race, going for the personal best, and playing with the boys, professionally and personally, had proved very rough indeed. I'd been in no way ready for the big time, the real deal.

Whatever ability I might have had to love and trust didn't survive the hardening of resolve that it took for me not to kill myself between 1974 and 1977. I ate yams, smoked pot, studied the stars, and hung on. I resolved to do what was necessary to survive in a society that made me feel like shit.

It was crystal clear to me, as Stokely Carmichael used to say, that I could no longer afford to be emotionally vulnerable, naively moral, romantic. That's what they had turned against me—my own idealistic humanism. I had suffered because I hadn't hated and despised enough, except myself for not being able to stand up under relentless torture. I wouldn't make that mistake again.

I had always been what some people said was "too" sensitive, though it seems to me you're either sensitive or you're not—no such thing as "too." Well, anyway, according to my sensitivity, we live in a world of atrocity, on the job, in the street, and at home.

My thirties were toilet paper, emotionally speaking. I established myself as a poet and editor, feature writer, then as a broadcaster. To an outsider those activities appeared to be career moves, but to me they were rehabilitation. I was reconstructing my world view and my self in light of the hard lessons experience had taught me thus far.

Ultimately, it took all my energy to keep a roof over my head. There was none left over for love. At last I had accepted my "place" among the poor and working-class, the dispossessed and downtrodden; among the folk whose struggle for survival teaches them skills for protecting and preserving themselves.

> *I am the downtrodden*
> *I am the poor and deprived*
> *that got star billing for a decade*
>
> *I am the snarl of Afro hair and mulatto mouth,*
> *a frantic dancer of defiance in my*
> *sun-raped wrappings reminiscent of some*
> *racial home denied me by the*
> *cataracts of time*
>
> *I am the mind that is a*
> *terrible thing to waste, the blacker berry*
> *with the sweeter juice, the Matriarch of*
> *impromptu families and the automatic suspect*
> *for light-fingered crimes*
> *mine is not a People of the Book/taxed but*
> *acknowledged; our distinctiveness is*
> *not yet a dignity; our Holocaust is lower case . . .*

Anything else had been a sham—all that boarding school finish, the exquisitely ladylike sensibilities and intellectual airs. None of that had kept me from being humiliated and crushed.

I had to learn how to intimidate and injure, how to get folk up offa me. I'm still working on it. I'm pleased to report progress since I was thirty. It's taken only another fifteen or so years of the life I'm running out of.

That comin'-round-forty fling I mentioned earlier was my last gasp of girlhood. I was taking a chance on love, as the song says, on that stupid, chump love so highly recommended for women. Yeah, I made him the center of my universe and that turned out to be as dumb as I'd always thought it would be, and as unrewarding as it has always been.

We had some great times, too, but, man, is the price ever too high. Sex ain't that compelling, and I keep cats for reciprocal companionship, so I can deal, even if I'd probably be less fat were I getting both from a good guy. But I'm not down for the emotional atrocities. I don't know any married people whom I envy. And I shall put no other gods before me.

The Act

Behind the Word

DORISJEAN AUSTIN

DorisJean Austin's retelling of the impact of rape on her life is a chilling reminder of female vulnerability and male corruption of power. It is also a composed, powerful affirmation of the female/human spirit's ability to heal, to forgive, and to grow. DorisJean recalls her rape, saying, "All the women in my family seem, to my recollection, to have been raped that night." This is a painful yet all too honest assertion of the sisterhood of oppression. And it reminds us that each time a woman is raped the world is less safe for every woman. The victim, her family, friends, even her community, suddenly call into question everything they once thought they knew about safety, innocence, guilt, shame, and justice.

For the victim the questions are very simple. If no one embraces you, how can you embrace yourself? If friends forsake you, how can you swear allegiance to who you are no matter what? When you are twelve and on the border between training bras and the arrival of your period and a man violates your body, ravishes your ability to trust, maybe you hide, maybe you take flight in your imagination, and run away, even when everyone thinks you are there. You run, perfecting the sprint, over time, over years, growing into a long-distance runner of the mind, and you run, but one day the memory catches you. And then . . .

"The Act"

"You can't tell me you don't hate men just a little."

This mystical assumption, in many forms, is a recurring proposal to the raped, by what I presume to be the unraped citizens. And it never fails to put me in a sardonic humor—a child on the outside, looking in, again.

As a woman, I've often wondered if all victims, during and after rape—both male and female—become voyeurs, locked into and away from the unbelievable trauma. I've looked at my own denial and I've wondered.

As a writer, I must consider resisting the seduction of words, denying myself the writer's hiding place of metaphor, paradigm, simile, because I know that for me, rape was nothing like *"breaking into a house,"* nor did it resemble *"a flower crushed before its bloom."* Although, perhaps, like Jean Toomer's character in his classic novel, *Cane:* As with *Karintha,* I recognize that, still, today, *"This interest of the male, who wishes to ripen a growing thing too soon, could mean no good to . . ."* I, too, am a storyteller. It is my safe place. So, to approach some understanding of the experience, to *see* the act behind the word, for my own protection, I reduce the act to story:

"The Story"

Over thirty years ago, when rape was still a capital *R* felony (the *R* in rape keeps getting smaller), it happened that a twelve-year-old girl came out of a hosiery store on an early Saturday evening onto a busy street in a small town in New Jersey where, without reason or warning, she was punched in her stomach by a young man who waited there. He seemed to her very tall. He forced her through the open door into the backseat of a parked car that held the driver and another male companion in the front and one other male in the backseat. The car took off. Ike and Tina Turner were singing "A Fool in Love" accompaniment for the ride, which stayed well within the speed limit as the car cruised up and down dusk-shadowed streets as streetlights came on. Her twelve-year-old neighbors were probably settling down after dinner, after washing dishes, maybe to watch "Captain Video" on the Du-Mont Television Network. The victim listened to Ike and Tina on the car radio. Throughout her life she would associate Tina Turner with the violent ride through familiar streets during those last minutes of her childhood when she was held by one man and raped by another.

Her rapist whispered threats about what would happen to her if she told anyone, what *he* would do to her if she told. He shook her shoulders roughly as one sometimes does to get a child's attention. He called her by name. She knew all four men. They were her neighbors. The one whispering in her ear was married, soon to become a father. The heady smell of sweet wine filled the backseat. The shock of it all forever dislodged her from the time fabric of the world of adolescence. She had no thoughts, no opinions, no voice. But she could hear: "*Turn on the lights, man,*" the one who was holding her wrists said. Those were the only words spoken while he held her wrists in his hands over her head, which also rested in his lap. This was no time to get a ticket, so he told the driver: "*Turn on the lights.*" Later that night, she would repeat the words to the detective at the police station. "He kept telling the driver to turn on the lights," she would tell him.

They didn't make her cry. They made her mother and her aunts cry. They made her younger sister cry, but she refused to cry—or to remember. She "forgot" the incident, locked it away for more than twenty years until it surfaced like one of those detailed instant replays at a football or basketball game. The encysted memory had, however, replayed itself in secret as it shaped the young woman in the girl.

When the details of that evening returned to me, I was in the bathtub almost catatonic with exhaustion. The memory had sprung loose from its trappings during the long process of mourning my mother's death the previous year; I had been defenseless against even small calamities since. Trains that were late and zippers that stuck reduced me to tears, exhaustion, then sleep. I had been hospitalized for "emotional exhaustion" brought on by grief.

The return of the memory of the scenes described here made me feel as if I'd been hit over the head with the swing of a home-run bat, catapulted me dripping from the tub back to my bedroom, then back to the bathroom for a towel. Then, trailing water, clutching a towel, back to the mirror in the bedroom to check my image, breathlessly mumbling "Good God!" over and over. I was afraid something was seriously wrong with my mind. This, I kept thinking, was surely not a forgettable event. Was this what my therapists had been looking for on my sporadic visits over the last decade? One doctor used the term "fractured personality" to describe me because in my conversations with him, in my

thoughts, dreams, and daydreams, I was exclusively *she* and *her*.
I've considered this imploded memory: Could it be fatal, like an
undetonated bomb from a forgotten war? After so long a time,
recall of my third-person adolescence felt normal. Until suddenly,
there it was, as clear as my wild face in the mirror: the act, from
start to finish; Bucky Davis, the detective who had to ask me
questions that visibly upset him; the police lineup; the police doctors with their painful shots to ensure immunity; the faces of my
mother, my two aunts, and later that night at home, my younger
sister. All the women in my family seem, to my recollection, to
have been raped that night.

I escaped when they stopped the car to change places. Both the
front and the back doors of the car were open on the curb side,
and he stood between the doors zipping up his pants. The young
man in the passenger seat in the front got out. It was his turn. The
hands that held my wrists during the act were now clutching only
the arms of my coat. I remember that coat well: a collarless green
Black Watch plaid, wool that flowed full from the shoulders. I
loved that coat. I slipped my arms from the sleeves, kicked the
back door wider open, and ran. I was in the middle of a quiet
two-lane boulevard. He actually had my coat in his hand coming
toward me. *"Come on and get your coat, girl. Nobody's going to believe
you, you know. Nobody!"* He laughed. That's when I started
screaming—as loud and as long as my breath allowed. There was a
little grocery store open on the other side of the street. A woman
came out. He dropped my coat in the street and jumped in the
car, and they took off. The woman's husband went and got my
coat from the middle of the street. The couple were old-world
Europeans with heavy accents. Their outrage and gentleness as-
sured me it was over. They took me into their store and called the
police. The husband leaned on the counter with one hand over
his face, I remember.

That Saturday evening I had gone to the store to buy my first pair
of nylon stockings to be worn to Monumental Baptist Church on

Sunday. Then, after church, to the Stanley, the State, or the Loews Theater, where I may have been meeting a boy by the water fountain. That's the way we practiced dating back then. My stockings were the symbol of relinquished childhood. The color I chose was called "Red Fox." They had black seams and black heels. My mother probably would not have let me wear them.

The rapists were picked up that night. At the lineup, I remember, my aunt, five feet of outraged Southern woman, beating them about the chest and face. They were handcuffed behind their backs. I don't remember which one she was assaulting. But I do remember the ensuing postponements of the trial because one or several of the defendants had "injured" themselves severely enough not to be able to make their appearance in court. It was rumored—and I choose to believe—that the community of male convicts saw no common bond between themselves and these child molesters and rapists. I was not, because of my age, made to testify in open court.

Before their conviction, the wife of the man who raped me came to my house. I was still home from school, convalescing. She came when my mother was at work. She wore a navy-blue double-breasted coat that was popular back then—chesterfields, they were called. She had on sunglasses. She was very pregnant. She wouldn't come into the house but rang the bell and waited downstairs on the front porch. The wife (I do remember her name, although I won't call it here) was soft, nonthreatening; she looked away while she spoke. She wanted to know from me if it was true. She was a short woman, and even then I towered over her. I think we were both close to tears. I couldn't talk, so I nodded, *Yes*. Something seemed to go out of her then. She didn't sag or anything. "Died a little," I think is appropriate: another rape victim.

Although the newspapers withheld my name, of course, the identity of the anonymous twelve-year-old in the headlines became known in spite of the assurances of the police, the doctors, my minister—my mother gave no assurances except her love. The unrelenting grief of the women in my family hinted at the effects of the "secret" in my community. My rapist's whispers were true. In that small New Jersey community I became guilty. The embarrassment of my preadolescent girlfriends brought about a silence that, in biblical parlance, "begat" my ostracism. My friends were unable to come to the telephone when I called. I believe it was the mothers' instructions that dictated the reactions of my former friends when I approached them around school grounds, on buses, and in stores. My wounded pride responded; I shunned them, became first angry, solitary, then, to hide my shame, enraged. The young men in my community were totally unable to cope with my new status and either refused to "see" me or swaggered around me in new roles with a new language that ill-fit them.

It was therefore surprising when the men in my community reacted to the rapists with such outrage. The only young man released on bail was horribly beaten by "assailants unknown" on the first day he returned to the streets of town. The women, on the other hand, displayed an embarrassed aversion that could easily be interpreted as shame. We were female, estranged and committed to guilty silence, together. In my house, I had forbidden anyone ever to mention it again. I refused the therapy suggested by the police; my mother allowed me.

When an editor friend of mine first asked me to write this article, I wasn't sure that I could. Over three decades had passed, and I still wasn't sure if I'd come far enough away to examine the details that I remember now like an old, often-seen motion picture. I was surprised at the lucid objectivity I felt when the story was finally committed to paper. The objectivity followed the event. Only that once in my life have I ever felt a personal reaction to these memories. I left myself—that self—when it happened to *her:* an overconfident, skinny twelve-year-old with a strident voice, who belted out hymns at Tuesday night choir practice, imitated her elders' flailings at Thursday night prayer meetings when the old folks "got religion," laughed too loud, cried copious tears at sad films, read insatiably—even during summer breaks from school. In 1991, part of my catharsis was to go on

"The Oprah Winfrey Show" with two other women who were also traumatized as children, who also blocked the memory until they were adults, able to survive the knowing. One young lawyer from California saw her father abuse and murder her young girl-friend when she was a child; the other woman buried Holocaust prison camp memories for decades. Actually, I find it fantastic that the human psyche can come to such immediate aid as total loss of memory to protect such young hosts as we were, for so long. Still, no matter how close I stand to this case, those memories belong to *her,* not to me. When rage surfaces, it is in principle, not in person, that I feel it at all.

For me, the healing process was a long one. Some unconscious recovery obviously went on during my "blackout," because I functioned well in many roles. Sporadically, I educated myself, married, divorced, married, divorced; but hindsight reveals that at some level, before I was thirteen years old, I began to run. Away? Toward some dimly perceived salvation? I don't know. But I do remember announcing that I would not in the future attend church. I demanded and was allowed to transfer from my school and go to another, out of my geographic zone. The special per-mission required was obtained and I entered the new school anon-ymously. I see the skinny, big-eyed girl belligerently avoiding contact with her Godless and absent adolescence. She was tough. She watched her own back. And she survived high school.

When I turned eighteen, I begged, coerced, and stormed the walls of my mother's resistance until she relented and permitted me to join the Women's Army Corps. If anything could wake me up, it should have been the army, for which I was totally unsuited, although I did begin my college education in the army. I was rigid and intractable, court-martialed for trying to escape—AWOL (Absent Without Leave), they called it. Shortly after that, I found out that a woman could get an early discharge if she had completed a minimum of one year of active duty, if she were married—and her husband objected to his wife being a soldier. Upon completing my first year of active duty, I met a soldier, fell

in love, became engaged, married, and, within months, with my
husband's authority, exercised my married woman's option to
become a civilian again. I returned to my mother's house with
scarcely a clue as to why I'd so urgently left, back full circle to
where I'd begun.

It was after my second divorce that I sought professional help.
Not for the rape I still did not remember, but for the senseless
running away, for the pain of my anxiety attacks that could send
me to bed for indefinite periods or to the hospital with blood
pressure soaring, and for depression so acute that two different
doctors, on separate occasions, diagnosed me as manic-depressive.
My recovery did not proceed with any speed until the day I could
tell my therapist, "I was raped when I was a child." That's when I
stopped running. I'd arrived at the end of that era of my life: a
nervous breakdown in a New York psychiatric hospital, trying to
heal the child I'd run away from.

That's the story.

The woman I became is, I know, often a volatile and *en garde*
human being, oversensitive to the possibility of attack. Often I
perceive danger when confronted by male anger. The thought of
physical threat evokes a well-rehearsed drama: I secretly cast myself in the image of Pallas Athene, patron goddess of the Women's
Army Corps, goddess of war and wisdom, who sprang, fully
armed from the head of Jupiter, a man-made mythical structure
conceived without a mother, or some equally fearsome and invio-
lable mythic construct.

And no, I do not hate men. Although I can't deny that the
experience did irrevocably alter my perceptions of them and me
and us and Thee. Somewhere, I abandoned my "understanding,"
as historically assigned to females, in perpetuity. Our bizarre com-
pliance with the male assignment of our "understanding"—never
to be mistaken for the male's powerful over-standing—in matters
of emotional, spiritual, physical, and sexual abuse is the saddest
kind of cowardice. We appear to fear beyond all reason to call the
male to accountability. It is not easy for me, today, nor do I

especially try to leave assumptions unchallenged, questions unan-
swered. On the subject of rape, I don't even try to resist the
imbecility of defending my child self and the woman I've become
against any suspicion that somehow girls, boys, women, and men
provoke the instance of their own sexual abuse and rape. I've
heard the whispers and the even louder voices. I am sure that as
you read this, some of you, a few of you, at least—I hope a
growing-smaller few of you—would like to know if, as a result of
this twelve-year old child's experience, I am constantly immersed
in a state of impotent rage, or locked in sophomoric self-pity. Am
I a *hopeless neurotic, maybe?, a dyke?, a lesbian?, a ball-breaker?, a
castrating black bitch?*

No. I am none of the above.

I am a writer.

And I constantly write myself sane again.

I am a woman.

Although I am never *just* a woman.

The simple fact is, I am awesome. To continue becoming
DorisJean Austin, Black woman writer in America, I had to first
become awesome: in my ability to survive, in my imagination, in
my ability to channel my rage positively and live in the greatest
quasi-health possible in our society, in my role of healer and self-
healer, in my generosity, my willingness to explore my pain and
heal myself, as women in this white male system have learned to
do for ourselves, each other, and our legion communities over the
centuries. To resist the seduction of the joyless victim's role—you
know, the music of *Invictus:* head bloody but unbowed. And write
it. I am only one, and I have survived many stories. Neither a
boast nor self-pity, these are facts—like the sun, the moon, the
wind, and rain, like Billie Holiday and those "Blue Monday"
mornings, like Audre Lorde's *Cancer Journals,* like the folks up the
street and the neighbors next door.

Like all of us, I had to learn to survive shocks. I have survived
many stories to become my own black self—and I am still becoming. Rape is one of my stories. It is only one of my most enraged
stories.

. . .

Hate men?

No, I do not hate men.

I do hate the lethargy in my society's response to the victims of rape. The crime and the perpetrators have the undivided attention of the media: the churches and the councils of churches; the analysts; the theorists; the criminologists; the scholars who join in debate on late-night television, long after the fact. Studies show that men and boys have been bullied into such sexual fear that they are even more hesitant than women to report, to reveal, to risk the ridicule inherent in becoming "guilty" of having been raped. These victims who, as one New York judge explained the lenience of his sentencing, ". . . *had not, after all, been chopped up or mutilated.*"

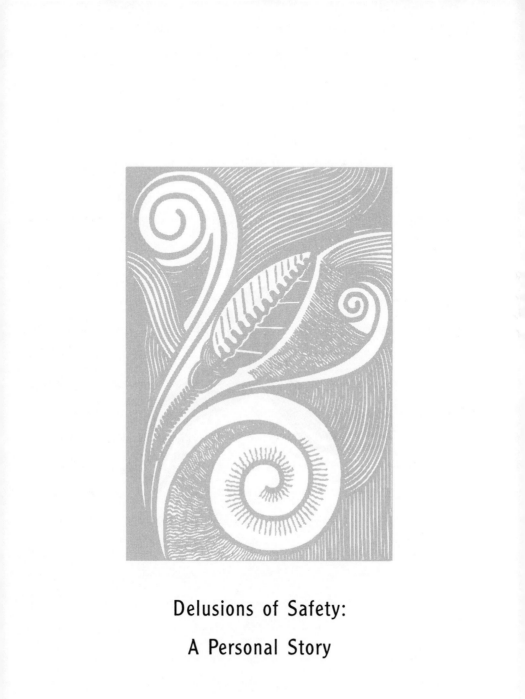

Delusions of Safety:

A Personal Story

MARCIA
ANN GILLESPIE

We have
a word for it now. Battering. But when I was a child, there were no
words. There were women like Mrs. Godwin, who lived in a neighbor's
rooming house, and who got a "Saturday night whipping" at the end of
each week when her husband came home, half his paycheck gone, drunk,
mean, and looking for his wife.

There weren't any words for it then, just women with bruised, purplish
cheeks and eyelids that forced everyone to turn away, embarrassed for the
women, belittled by their own fear of or inability to scream at her man,
Shame! Shame!

There were no words for it then, just a belief everybody, even women,
paid homage to, that, If he beat her that bad, she must've done something
to deserve it. There were no words then, but the silence around us said,
She's HIS woman, and besides a man's got a right. We have a word for it
now. But men still feel they've got the right.

A memory:
I am eight, maybe nine, years old; it's a hot summer Sunday afternoon; family and friends have gathered at my maternal grandmother's. The adults are sitting around the table talking as adults always seemed to do. My best friend Adrienne and I are sitting on the high front porch, shaded by climbing roses and trumpet vines. Legs dangling off the side, oblivious to the admonitions not to mess up our good clothes, half listening to the music welling up and out of the Baptist church, the sounds of people shouting and clapping to the pounding piano, we are eating strawberry ice cream and sharing secrets when the screams begin.

I can hear the woman pleading, begging him not to hit her again, saying, "I'm sorry, baby, I'm sorry." The man cursing, threatening to "beat the shit out of you, bitch." Then the sound of her wailing pierces the afternoon. People gather on porches and at windows. And suddenly the two of them are in the street, just a few yards away, she running from him, he in hot, drunken pursuit. Someone yells that they've called the cops; still, he grabs her, one hand in her hair dragging her back, the other punching her. Then someone shouts, "She has a knife!" And suddenly he bellows as blood shoots from his chest. The blood immobilizes him and galvanizes her—cursing, she wrests loose and weaves around him, slashing his face, his arms, his sides. Blood spurts, pooling at their feet. She stands panting, her swollen eyes fixed on the knife, when the police finally arrive. He stands weaving, touching himself, looking at his bloody hands, repeating in disbelief, "Bitch, you stabbed me, you cut me, bitch."

What happened that long-ago Sunday ended as quickly as some summer storms. I ate my ice cream the entire time, and when my friend, sickened by the bloodshed, pushed hers aside, I finished that as well. Where I grew up violence was often played out in public view. People got shot, stabbed, bludgeoned, and beaten; a few of them died. I witnessed the rage, heard the cursing, screams, deadly silences, saw the way blood spurts and runs while I was still a braided, beribboned little girl.

But that particular incident is the one that remains vivid. What happened that day was not typical. Despite the stories that my folks tell—about the women who could and did beat any man walking—most times women were left broken and bleeding. Growing up, though, I felt safe in that small neighborhood. The violence was predictable. It went with full moons, heat waves, grinding oppression, and the stuff of the blues—poverty, hopelessness, drunkenness, rage, foolin' around with other folks' stuff, meanness, feuds, and revenge. It happened to unchurched wild livers, Saturday night bingers who spent their week's wages in bars and their guilt and frustrations on each other. It didn't happen to nice girls from God-fearing homes, wasn't done by our brothers, boyfriends, and fathers. No! No! No! Or so you were told by adults you trusted.

I was in college when I learned that it didn't just happen in certain places, to certain people. My boyfriend knocked me down a short flight of stairs. I'd embarrassed him by slipping away from a party to check out some other guys. We argued and then he punched me and I went sprawling on the stairs. I'd never been hit by a male person before—nor since. He'd never hit a female person before, don't know if he has since. I was lucky; other than a slight bruise on my face, I was not hurt. We were both shocked by his violence. He cried and apologized. Shaken, spitting mad, and frightened, though I pretended not to be, I made a very big scene, then quit him.

My father once said, "If a man hits you once, he'll hit you again. The first time he'll say he's sorry. He may even cry. But he'll do it again, with less provocation." The words made little impression, since I couldn't imagine ever being with a man who'd lay a hand on me. But having crossed through the looking glass once, I never wanted to fall through again. I quickly ended relationships with men who had short tempers, or who in any way crowded me physically. I tried to stick close to the rules: Avoid arguments. If you argue, make sure it doesn't get out of control. Don't publicly disagree with your man. Don't draw undue attention. Don't juggle men, but if you do, exercise utmost stealth and guile, or else let each one know that he isn't the only one on your dance card.

But the rules never seem to hold. You have opinions. You are independent. You live in the world. You're educated, successful, and so are your friends. You go to parties and bars. You meet guys, exchange numbers, make dates. You travel. You talk to strangers. You're streetwise. You can take care of yourself. And in your own kitchen during a party when a guy who's had too much to drink starts to make threatening moves, you grab a hot frying pan filled with grease, scare him sober, and stop him cold. You scare the hell out of yourself as well. But still you want to believe you're safe, that those two incidents were aberrations, nothing more.

And then one night you find yourself half hanging out a window, twenty-two stories up, held there by the man you've been involved with for months. How can this be happening to you? You who perfected your cool-down procedures, who know how to avoid the ones who might lay hands on you. How can he be doing this? He's a television news reporter! One minute you were out laughing and drinking, the next you're in his apartment and he's screaming that you were hitting on his friends. You protest. One minute you're halfway out the door, the next you're half out the window, pleading and praying.

I was twenty-four when that happened. We'd met at a journalists' meeting. Our relationship had been easy and delicious. He was smart, funny, and very gentle. We'd rarely argued, and then it was never personal. He'd seemed in the best of humor that night, up until the moment we walked into his apartment. And then Dr.

Jekyll turned into Mr. Hyde. To this day I'm not sure what triggered it—or why he pulled me back inside. I know that as soon as my feet hit the floor, I grabbed my bag and started running out the door. All I wanted was to put as much distance as possible between me and that moment of sheer terror.

I never told my family, never reported it to the police. And when I spoke about it to my best friends, I tended to make light of the incident. I also went into hiding for a while. Didn't date. Avoided places we knew in common. When we were in the same room, I kept my distance.

He was crazy, I had no doubt about that. What worried me was that my early warning system had failed to detect it. I vowed to exercise greater care, by checking a guy out.

You know the drill, I'm sure. You subtly grill him about who he knows, where he's been. You ask your friends about him. You ask them to ask around. You never come out and say I want to find out if this man is a bully, if he beats women. And you probably don't even admit what you're doing yourself. Time passes, memories fade, none of the men you meet show any Hyde-like leanings. At the very worst the reports you get, when you remember to ask, say things like he's difficult, a dog when it comes to women, self-centered, a con artist, a lousy lover, or still hung up on someone else. Sometimes you drop him. Other times you proceed with caution.

Caution, now there's a word. Being cautious becomes almost second nature to women. Keep your legs closed, skirts down, eyes demure; don't talk to strange men. All those rules that tell us to keep to our place, don't rock the boat, don't be a wild child. Or else you'll be vulnerable, unprotected, and ultimately some man's prey. It comes with the morning paper and the evening news. A woman murdered, raped, beaten, tortured. She's single, she's married. She's prepubescent, she's pregnant. She's a senior citizen. She lives in the city, in the suburbs, in the country. She's rich, poor, middle-class, working-class, unemployed. She's a student, a nun, an investment broker, a schoolteacher, a full-time homemaker, a factory worker, retired. She was home, in her car, on the job, in an elevator, on a subway, bus, walking, jogging. She was alone, with her husband, lover, friends. She was with her children. He was someone she knew. He was a stranger. He stalked her. He stumbled upon her. He didn't even know her name. He was not alone.

You try not to think too much about it. You decide not to read the papers. Or maybe you check each report closely, hoping to be reassured in some way—that the crime didn't happen in your neighborhood, where you work, shop, or travel. Perhaps like one of my coworkers you study them to see if there's something you can learn, some precaution you need to take, some habit you need to break in order to keep yourself safe. When photos of the men's faces appear, you study them, searching for some clue. Serial murderers, rapists, batterers, sadists, and killers should look different from the men we know, love, laugh, work, and live with.

When do you finally realize that he doesn't have a face any different from your brother's, lover's, son's, or friend's? How long does it take for that knowledge to sink in and then what do you do, how do you live with it?

I came to that realization shortly after my twenty-seventh birthday. The man I was involved with had given me a huge party to celebrate. Friends, acquaintances, and even folks I didn't know turned up. It was terrific. Three weeks later two detectives arrived at my office. They showed me the photograph of a woman, young and pretty. They asked if I recognized her. I didn't. They told me her name, said she lived in my neighborhood, that she'd been at my birthday party. As I looked at her smiling face in that photograph, they told me that she'd been sexually assaulted and murdered in her apartment, slashed and stabbed, her head nearly severed from her body. Then they informed me that they believed she'd met the murderer at my party, and they asked me for a list of all the men who were there.

I remember shaking my head saying, "Oh, no, there has to be some kind of mistake." And the hard, flat voice of the detective cutting me off: "Her last known conversation was on the phone to a girlfriend. She told her friend she was getting ready to go out with a guy she met at your party. She'd started to go into more detail when she said, 'Listen, that's my bell, it must be him. I'll call you tomorrow.' She was dead within a few hours."

That night my guy and I sat up late talking. Distrustful of the police, shocked, not wanting to believe it was possible, we slowly wrote down the names of the men we'd invited, the men we remembered being there, the friends who'd brought men we didn't know. Separately, together, with the police and on our own, we went over that list as it steadily grew from thirty to sixty. The police asked us not to talk about the investigation. Weeks went by, friends would say they'd been questioned. Every day I'd scour the papers looking to see if an arrest had been made. Unable to bear the not knowing, I called one of the detectives. He said that two of the men from our list were still under suspicion. He wouldn't say who they were. When I called again two months later, he told me he believed one of them was the murderer, but that there wasn't enough evidence to charge him.

That happened nineteen years ago. Men I would normally have dated were at that party. We all moved in the same circles. Yet when they called to ask me out I backed away. There were a few exceptions: one man who I knew had been on another continent when the murder occurred. And a couple of others I felt drawn to —so I prevailed upon that detective to check the files and say yes or no. But how many times can you call the police to ask if a guy you'd like to date was one of the two prime suspects in a murder? Besides, the case got filed, the detective transferred, and I exercised a form of selective amnesia.

Do you remember the game from childhood where you drew a circle in the dirt or on the sidewalk, called it home, then stepped inside, where no one could get you, because you were safe? I believe we women are in a constant process of drawing and redrawing that circle, having made one more adjustment in our lifestyles in the hope of coming home safe. Whether we admit it or not, we know that little more than fate keeps us from becoming one of the statistics. We adopt ever more complex maneuvers, all the while clinging to the belief that what we're doing is perfectly normal behavior and not the well-honed survival tactics of a group under siege. Nor do we stop to consider freedoms we lose as part of the escalating price of safety, no matter how marginal.

It's horrible thinking of yourself as vulnerable, that each time you walk out your door some violent HE may be waiting. That the man you meet for dinner tonight may assume he has unlimited rights to the use of your body. That the man you know as warm, funny, and kind may one day turn around and slam his fist into your skull, throw you against a wall or down a flight of stairs. That your husband, lover, son, or brother may be a terrorist in waiting. Most of us will say that can't be true, or that it's impossible to live with that kind of suspicion hovering. We master our fear, call on reservoirs of faith, and refuse to let the doubts control us. And we pretend that nothing is amiss. We keep redrawing those circles. What we do—what I do—is keep on keeping on.

I don't eat strawberry ice cream anymore.

Wounded in
the House of a Friend

SONIA SANCHEZ

Sonia Sanchez *spins a blues/rap meditating on adultery, love, and lust. How is it that you always know when you are sharing your man? When he strays? When he tips? The extrasensory perception endowed by personal histories carved in blood, sweat, and stone is at the heart of Sanchez's moody, electric musings. She pulls the slender thread of trust that binds lovers and chokes them when it breaks.*

S*et no. 1*

*The unspoken word
is born, i see it in our
eyes dancing*

She hadn't found anything. I had been Careful. No lipstick. No matches from a well-known bar. No letters. Cards. Confessing an undying love. Nothing tangible for her to hold on to. But I knew she knew. It had been on her face, in her eyes for the last nine days. It was the way she looked at me sideways from across the restaurant table as she picked at her brown rice sushi. It was the way she paused in profile while inspecting my wolf-dreams. It was the way her mouth took a detour from talk. And then as we exited the restaurant she said it quite casually: I know there's another woman. You must tell me about her when we get home.

Yeah. There was another woman. In fact there were three women. In Florida, California, and North Carolina. Places to replace her cool detachment of these last years. No sex for months. Always tired or sick or off to some conference designed to save the world from racism or extinction. If I had jerked off one more time in bed while lying next to her, it woulda dropped off. Still I wondered how she knew.

am i dressed right for the smoke
will it wrinkle if i fall?

i had first felt something was wrong at the dinner party. His colleague's house. He was so animated. The first flush of his new job i thought. He spoke staccato style. Two drinks in each hand. His laughter. Wild. Hard. Contagious as shrines. Enveloped the room. He was so wired that i thought he was going to explode. i didn't know the people there. They were all lawyers. Even the wives were lawyers. Glib and self-assured. Discussing cases, and colleagues. Then it happened. A small hesitation on his part. In answer to a question as to how he would be able to get some important document from one place to another, he looked at the host and said: They'll get it to me. Don't worry. And the look passing back and forth between the men told of collusion and omission. Told of dependence on other women for information and confirmation. Told of nights i had stretched out next to him and he was soft. Too soft for my open legs. And i turned my back to him and the nites multiplied out loud. As i drove home from the party i asked him what was wrong? What was bothering him? Were we okay? Would we make love tonite? Would we ever make love again? Did my breath stink? Was i too short? Too tall? Did i talk too much? Should i wear lipstick? Should i cut my hair? Let it grow? What did he want for dinner tomorrow nite? Was i driving too fast? Too slow? What is wrong man? He said: i was always exaggerating. Imagining things. Always looking for trouble.

Do they have children?
one does.

Are they married?
one is.

They're like you then.
yes.

How old are they?
Thirty-two, thirty-three, thirty-four.

What do they do?
An accountant and two lawyers.

They're like you then.
yes.

Do they make better love than i do?
I'm not answering that.

Where did you meet?
when I traveled on the job.

Did you make love in hotels?
yes.

Did you go out together?
yes.

To Bars? To Movies? To restaurants?
yes.

Did you make love to them all nite?
yes.

And then got up to do your company work?
yes.

*And you fall asleep on me right after dinner. After work. After
walking the dog.*
yes.

Did you buy them things?
yes.

Do you talk on the phone with them every day?
yes.

Do you tell them how unhappy you are with me and the children?
yes.

*Do you love them? Did you say that you loved them while making
love?*
I'm not answering that.

Can i pull my bones
together while skeletons
come out of my head?

i am preparing for him to come home. i have exercised. Soaked in the
tub. Scrubbed my body. Oiled myself down. What a beautiful day it's
been. Warmer than usual. The cherry blossoms on the drive are blooming
prematurely. The hibiscus are giving off a scent around the house. i have
gotten drunk off the smell. So delicate. So sweet. So loving. i have been
sleeping, no daydreaming all day. Lounging inside my head. i am walking
up this hill. The day is green. All green. Even the sky. i start to run
down the hill and i take wing and begin to fly and the currents turn me
upside down and i become young again childlike again ready to participate
in all children's games.

She's fucking my brains out. I'm so tired I just want to put my
head down at my desk. Just for a minute. What is wrong with her?
For one whole month she's turned to me every night. Climbed
on top of me. Put my dick inside her and become beautiful.
Almost birdlike. She seemed to be flying as she rode me. Arms
extended. Moving from side to side. But my God. Every night.
She's fucking my brains out. I can hardly see the morning and I'm
beginning to hate the night.

He's coming up the stairs. i've opened the venetian blinds. i love to see
the trees outlined against the night air. Such beauty and space. i have
oiled myself down for the night. i slept during the day. He's coming up
the stairs. i have been waiting for him all day. i am singing a song i
learned years ago. It is pretty like this nite. Like his eyes.

I can hardly keep my eyes open. Time to climb out of bed. Make the 7:20 train. My legs and bones hurt. I'm outta condition. Goddamn it. She's turning my way again. She's smiling. Goddamn it.

What a beautiful morning it is. i've been listening to the birds for the last couple hours. How beautifully they sing. Like sacred music. i got up and exercised while he slept. Made a cup of green tea. Oiled my body down. Climbed back into bed and began to kiss him all over . . .

Ted. Man. I'm so tired I can hardly eat this food. But I'd better eat cuz I'm losing weight. You know what man. I can't even get a hard-on when another bitch comes near me. Look at that one there with that see-through skirt on. Nothing. My dick is so limp only she can bring it up. And she does. Every nite. It ain't normal, is it, for a wife to fuck like she does. Is it man? It ain't normal. Like it ain't normal for a woman you've lived with for twenty years to act like this.

She was Killing him. He knew it. As he approached their porch he wondered what it would be tonite. The special dinner. The erotic movie. The whirlpool. The warm oil massage until his body awakened in spite of himself. In spite of an eighteen-hour day at the office. As he approached the house he hesitated. He had to stay in control tonite. This was getting out of hand.

She waited for him. In the bathroom. She'd be waiting for him when he entered the shower. She'd come in to wash his back. Damn these big walk-in showers. No privacy. No time to wash yourself and dream. She'd come with those hands of hers. Soaking him. On the nipples. Chest. Then she'd travel on down to his thing. His sweet peter jesus. So tired. So forlorn. And she'd begin to tease him. Play with him. Suck him until he rose up like some fucking private first class. Anxious to do battle. And she watched him rise until he became Captain Sweet Peter. And she'd climb on him. Close her eyes.

honey, it's too much you know.
What?

All this sex. It's getting so I can't concentrate.
Where?

At the office. At lunch. On the train. On planes. All I want to
do is sleep.
Why?

You know why. Every place I go you're there. Standing there.
Smiling. Waiting, touching.
Yes.

In bed. I can't turn over and you're there. Lips open. Smiling,
all revved up.
Aren't you horny too?

Yes. But enough's enough. You're my wife. It's not normal to
fuck as much as you do.
No?

It's not, well, nice, to have you talk the way you talk when
we're making love.
No?

Can't we go back a little, go back to our normal life when you
just wanted to sleep at nite and make love every now and then?
Like me.
No.

What's wrong with you. Are you having a nervous breakdown
or something?
No.

if i become the
other woman will i be
loved like you loved her?

And he says i don't laugh. All this he says while he's away in California for one week. But i've been laughing all day. All week. All year. i know what to do now. i'll go outside and give it away. Since he doesn't really want me. My love. My body. When he makes love his lips swell up. His legs and arms hurt. He coughs. Drinks water. Develops a strain at his butt-hole. Yeah. What to do now. Go outside and give it away. Pussy. Sweet. Black Pussy. For sale. Wholesale pussy. Right here. Sweet black pussy. Hello there Mr. Mailman. What's your name again? Oh yes. Harold. Can i call you Harry? How are you this morning? Would you like some cold water it's so hot out there. You want a doughnut a cookie some cereal some sweet black pussy? Oh God. Man. Don't back away. Don't run down the steps. Oh my God he fell. The mail is all over the sidewalk. hee. hee. hee. Guess i'd better be more subtle with the next one. hee. hee. hee. He's still running down the block. Mr. Federal Express Man. C'mon over here. Let me Fed Ex you and anyone else some Sweet Funky Pure Smelling Black Pussy. hee. hee. hee.

i shall become his collector of small things; become the collector of his burps, biceps, and smiles. i shall bottle his farts, frowns, and creases. i shall gather up his moans, words, outbursts. Wrap them in blue tissue paper. Get to know them. Watch them grow in importance. File them in their place in their scheme of things. i shall collect his scraps of food. Ferret them among my taste buds. Allow each particle to saunter into my cells. All aboard. Calling all food particles. C'mon board this fucking food express. Climb into these sockets golden with brine. i need to taste him again.

You can't keep his dick in your purse

Preparation for the trip to Dallas. Los Angeles. New Orleans. Baltimore. Washington. Hartford. Brownsville. Orlando. Miami. *Latecheckin. Rush. Limited liability.* That's why you missed me at the airport. Hotel. Bus stop. Train station. Restaurant. *Latecheckin. Rush. Limited liability.* I'm here at the justice in the eighties conference with lawyers and judges and other types advocating abbreviating orchestrating mouthing fucking spilling justice in the bars. Corridors. Bedrooms. Nothing you'd be interested in. *Luggage received damaged. Torn. Broken. Scratched. Dented. Lost.* Preparation for the trip to Chestnut Street. Market Street. Pine Street. Walnut Street. Locust Street. Lombard Street. *Earlycheckin. Slow and easy liability.* That's why you missed me at the office. At the office. At the office. It's a deposition I'm deposing an entire office of women and other types needing my deposing. Nothing of interest to you. A lot of questions no answers. Long lunches. Laughter. Penises. Flirtings. Touches. Drinks. Cunts and Coke. Jazz and Jacuzzis. *Morning. Evening. Received. Damaged. Torn. Broken. Dented. Scratched. Lost.*

I shall become a collector of me.

I shall become a collector of ME.
I SHALL become a collector of ME.
I shall BECOME a collector of ME.
I shall become A COLLECTOR of ME.
I SHALL BECOME a collector OF ME.
I shall become a collector of ME.
And put meat on my soul.

S*et no. 2*

i've been keeping company, with the layaway man
i say, i've been keeping company, with the layaway man
each time he come by, we do it on the installment plan

every Friday night, he come walking up to my do'
i say, every Friday night he come, walking up to my do'
empty pockets hanging, right on down to the floor

gonna get me a man, who pays for it up front
i say, gonna get me a man, who pays for it up front
cuz when i needs it, can't wait 'til the middle of next month

i been keeping company, with the layaway man
i say, i been keeping company, with the layaway man
each time he come by, we do it on the installment plan
each time he come by, we do it on the installment plan

In the Wink of an Eye:
Black Lesbians and Gay Men
Together

JEWELLE GOMEZ

*F*or gay
men and women, forging alliances, shaping friendships with one another,
is an often harrowing, but fulfilling journey. Shattering "traditional"
notions of sexuality, maleness, femaleness, makes the need for platonic
bonds that cross gender no less necessary or important.

In the lives, the faces, the dreams of her gay brothers, Jewelle Gomez
has found a reflection, a refinement of herself, both hidden and revealed.

To discover the meaning of her friendships with Black gay men, Jewelle
Gomez circled back in memory. There she found the seeds of her ability to
cross the great sexual divide. It all began with "Duke," her father, who
also happened to be her best friend.

Saturdays were father's day for me during my teen years. Living separately, with only assigned weekends in which to play father/daughter, Duke and I made the shape of our relationship through tasks and conversation. I loved the sound of clinking change, cascades of silver—quarters, nickels, and dimes—my father's tips from the Regent, the corner bar where he worked as bartender. He counted them out on his glass-topped desk, lining them up neatly, then grandly sweeping a share off into my hand. He made a jolly ritual of this payment for my dusting his record collection. And we bartered—he teaching me "mixology," me tutoring him in the high school Spanish I was learning. We discussed jazz and blues singers and his eclectic selection of books and magazines that included James Baldwin, Radclyffe Hall, *Jet,* and *Yachting.* These were my education. Just as important, they taught me who my father was—a man of immense curiosity and charm, erudition and wit. I listen for him when I try to create male characters in my fiction and look for him in all of my friends.

In retrospect, one of the most distinctive things about him seems to have been his genuine enjoyment of the company of women. Of course, he was a sharp dresser and attracted women as if he were Brook Benton. In fact, many of the neighborhood kids used to call him Jackie Gleason because of his great size, classy wardrobe, and sense of humor. His sensuality was apparent in both the easy way he wore his elegance and the soft roll of his eyes; in the subtlety of his social observations and the belly-laugh timbre of his jokes.

But he actually enjoyed us—me, my stepmother, my grandmother. He loved talking with us, listening to our stories, watching television with us, making us laugh. It was not just something
he had to do, or an alternative when "the guys" couldn't be
around. He fit in. He could be with women and not have to prove
he was a "man." If my stepmother gave my cousins spankings
when they misbehaved you could see great tears roll down his
bronze cheeks, shamelessly. Yet it was his name we all used as a
warning—"If you don't stop eating my ice cream I going to tell
Duke!" No one could ever remember being punished by him but
the invocation of his name worked because we adored him and
wanted him to respect us. He didn't even relegate children to that
mindless toy box that most adults, especially adult males, usually
resort to. He had no difficulty looking any of us in the eye. The
women of my family were independent, forward-thinking, expansive, passionate storytellers and Duke fit in. He was happy to be
their equal.

As the years pass, I'm not certain if it's simply my getting older
or that the times are changing but it has become harder to find
Duke in male friends. Each year the black men I know express
more bitterness, less hope. There are many valid reasons, of
course. Much is made of "manhood" in this culture, and the
subtle ways that black men are told they will never be good
enough are stunning. I see it every day. I've worked in administra-
tive jobs for the past fifteen years of my life and it continues to
provoke a visceral pain inside me when I see the disdain directed
toward black men delivering packages. No matter the age, or state
of dress, they are invisible to white people. This is certainly a
question of class as well as race, but the "manness" of black men
seems only recognizable as a threat in this culture.

I worked for an advertising company for many years and I
developed a friendly familiarity with the regular messengers who
were black. When a white coworker heard one messenger inviting
me to a musical event in which he was performing, she acted as if
I'd been conversing with my typewriter table. Not shocked but
confused, unable to imagine this black messenger was also a man,

that he had a life with aspirations and connections to something other than his bicycle and her packages. She also seemed incredulous that I, who'd been lifted up from what she seemed to perceive as the mire of blackness and blessed with a career, might feel connected to this messenger. She questioned me insistently, barely waiting for him to get out the door.

Today, more and more, that common bond between me and black men seems stretched thin. It is balanced less on personal interactions, like the wry wink the messenger returned to give me behind my coworker's back, and more on vaguely remembered historical events. The sixties was a time when we had official titles: "Brother" and "Sister," as if to negate all the other names slave owners had given us—mammy, uncle, Remus, Beulah. When I talk with heterosexual black men we speak of The Movement as if it were a shared adolescence that makes us siblings for life. But like any vision of the past it's never exactly the same in everyone's memory. And my assessment of the disadvantages to being a woman within the context of the Civil Rights and Black Power Movements is certainly different from that of my brothers. None of them seem to remember H. Rap Brown's heartily greeted pronouncement that "the only position for women in The Movement is prone."

Feminism has not taken away my pleasure at the hope which that period signified for me but it does require me to insist that both political consciousness and action be more comprehensive this time. In the nineties I demand that my brothers look past rhetoric and see me.

With our past in deep shadow it is increasingly more difficult to find the shared contemporary experiences or opinions that might help me as a black woman work with black men to shape a bright future. There were always several groupings of black men with which I was never able to make serious connection. In college there were the strivers, those whom I suspected would drop "the community" as soon as the right job came along. I could always recognize them by the elaborate efforts they made to keep their dashikis well pressed. I grew up in a tenement in Boston, living on welfare with my great-grandmother. I wanted crisp pleats and the right job as much as anyone, yet their attitude reeked of escape rather than social consciousness.

Recently I heard a brother talking about finding a parking garage for his BMW as if that were a political triumph. He'd proudly maneuvered the baroque racism of corporate real estate in New York City and I felt as if the beautiful sweat on the face of Fannie Lou Hamer had been rendered invisible. I knew he and I had taken different paths that were unlikely to ever meet. And on an East Coast campus I was visiting to do a reading, deliver a lecture, and meet with some of the writing students, the Famous Black Writer in residence didn't bother to show up. One of his black female students told me not to take it personally, he never came to the readings that women writers did.

When I heard, in the fall of 1991, that Spike Lee had begun his much-publicized course on black film at Harvard by initially neglecting to include a film by a single black woman, I wasn't even surprised. In this case, as in the others, I felt as if an artificial construction—economics, academia—had rendered me superfluous to black male ego. I knew Duke would have been sorely disappointed in Spike, though. As he would with black men who feel duty-bound on public streets to comment on women's body parts. Or those who call black women "out of their names," as we used to say. Or those who must trash other ethnic groups to feel like men. There's a level of solipsism pervading black male culture in the U.S. that Duke would never tolerate and I still find myself surprised to see it.

Some of my heterosexual black male friends seem to have escaped the curse of culture and chromosomes. Clayton, a writer, has known me since I was in college, when he was a struggling with his own career. Over the years he's offered the most consistent, uncondescending encouragement for my writing, acting as an editor of my early clumsy efforts while he wrote for the *New York Times*. He never appeared threatened by my attempts to catch up with him. Another good friend, Morgan, stuck by me in the deep emotional clinches that men aren't generally trained for:

when my great-grandmother died, when I was out of work in New York City, when I couldn't figure out what to do next. He was managing a New York acting career, not the most lucrative undertaking for a black man in this country. But he offered himself and his family as a support system while I thrashed about trying not to drown.

In the mid-seventies I think both Clayton and Morgan, unlike many of my other straight black friends, saw my coming out as a lesbian as a new aspect of me; perhaps a surprising revelation but not an invasion by an alien being. They weren't afraid to like me even if it wasn't all about sex. These Brothers took their title seriously. It was their friendship that kept my eyes open for the black gay brothers I knew had to be out there somewhere.

In the glitter ball, disco world of the seventies it was difficult to connect with them through the light shows and quadrophonic sound systems. But as with Clayton and Morgan it was through the intense personal aspirations—theater and writing—that I first caught the subtle gay winks of black men, thrown past unsuspecting heterosexuals, that let me know there was a community. The first time I remember trying to make a social contact as a black lesbian it was with black gay men, actors who worked with me on a variety of productions in black theater. I would casually mention the name of a gay club like The Garage and we'd glance at each other to check the response. Then, as with the wink from the black messenger, we'd confirm our unity.

Until the mid-eighties the worlds of lesbians and gay men remained relatively separate. Except for the annual pride marches held around the country, we shared few cultural events, clubs, or political activities. But for black lesbians and gay men the world was not as easily divided. The history of oppression remained in our consciousness, even with some who were too young to really remember The Movement. And since we often were not accepted fully into the white gay world we frequently socialized with each other. We hung together in the corner at the cast parties and invited each other over for holiday dinners, knowing the food would taste just like home.

When I went on the first national gay march on Washington I had to be at the bus leaving Greenwich Village at 5 A.M. I slept on Rodney's couch, around the corner from the meeting place. We'd come out to each other years before when he was acting in a play I stage-managed. I was fascinated by his midwestern blackness and the way he paid attention when people talked to him, just like my father. I think he found my Bostonian manners and the rough ways of the theater a funny combination. We sat up talking most of the night, mainly about our lover relationships and what it was like to be black and gay in the New York theater world. It was a world of contradictions where gay men and lesbians were fanatically closeted and heterosexuals were vying to see who could be the most iconoclastic and arty. When I left Rodney's house before dawn we hugged and kissed goodbye and I remembered how much I'd missed black men since I'd stopped sleeping with them.

In reflecting on my friendships with black men in general and black gay men, what is always at issue for me, whether conscious or not, is how they view black women. That, of course, is an excellent indicator of how a man thinks of himself. And my great-grandmother always told me never keep company with a man who doesn't think much of himself. That the sexual tension between men and women is largely eliminated between gay men and lesbians allows, I think, an opportunity for both to really see and think about each other rather than reacting in socially prescribed ways. With straight friends like Morgan, Clayton, and later with gay friends like Rodney I'm drawn to their ability to actually see me, not just see a woman as an object. They perceive my professionalism, intellect, and passion. And in turn they share their own attributes with me rather than trying to use them to dominate me.

And then there's the unexpected pleasure of being able to view the object created by this culture—"woman"—alongside a man. It has been liberating to see another friend, Dan, let go of the strictures put on maleness and indulge in femaleness. We go through black magazines and scream at the brown-skin cartoon fashion figures because we know how far both of us are from that fake ideal—me with my size 16 figure and graying hair; he with hair everywhere. Dan dresses up in the very things that made me feel inadequate, the things I broke free of: heels, sequins, makeup. In doing so he has helped to create a space where we both can step back and see ourselves as separate from society's constructs of gender. From our perspective the idealized glossy photographs as well as the other misleading clues about who women and men should be are reduced to their meaningless size.

Because neither of us would give up our blackness, even if it were possible, both of us can paint and primp, don the masks, and laugh at whatever society imagines we both are. We share the wink behind the backs of both the straight and the black worlds. It's a special bond forged for me only with black gay men; a bond not broken in history by a slaver's lash or today by the disapproving sounds of air sucked through teeth.

For many years I've been going to concerts by the Lavender Light Black and People of All Color Gospel Choir. It's a lesbian and gay group that renders the songs of the gospel tradition in the most vibrant and moving ways I've experienced in years. What I see when I sit in the audience watching the black men I know, Charles, Lidell, others, is an abiding respect for our tradition and our survival. They sway in robes I'd recognize anywhere, yet there is that extra movement, giving just a bit more to the spirit. And that extra beat signifies an insistence that the tradition can be carried on by all of us, not just heterosexuals or the black, closeted "choir queens." Charles and Lidell prefer to commune with their people and their God out in the open.

And although the sexual tension may not be there between us what is allowed to flourish is the sensuality. When I'm with black men we revel in the *feel* of being brothers and sisters. We talk that talk, and walk that walk together. There is a sensuous texture to black life: the music, the use of words, the sensory pleasures of food, dance. We appreciate these things with each other. The commonality of our past and the linking of our future make the bond sensual and passionate even when it's not sexual.

I spent an afternoon riding the train up from Washington,

D.C., with poet Essex Hemphill and we both were surprised at the unexpected opportunity to talk for a couple of hours without interruption. When the train pulled out the conversation started with "Girrrrl . . ." in that drawn-out way we can say and rolled through the writing of Audre Lorde, Cheryl Clarke, and James Baldwin, the U.S. economy, the treachery of politicians, Luther Vandross, disco, white people in general and a few specific ones we knew, and broken hearts. We touched these things that have deep meaning for us in an unguarded way, using the familiar gestures and music of our fathers, mothers, and grandmothers. It was a synergy not so different from my heartfelt conversations with my best friend, Gwen, when we were in high school. And it felt much like those exuberant moments when my father and I talked about books and music. Essex and I revealed ourselves to each other as writers, as a man and a woman, as brother and sister. We took each other in unreservedly. And we had barely begun before the train pulled into the station and we kissed goodbye.

And now AIDS. The first black man I knew to die from HIV-related illness was Robert, a black actor. He'd done a lot of television, "Kojak" and other series, and some small parts in films. But onstage he was a tall bundle of American/African energy, large eyes, dark, slightly wavey hair cut close, and mocha skin.

In a play by Adrienne Kennedy (*A Movie Star Has to Star in Black and White*) at the Public Theater his character was on a hospital gurney during the entire performance, and even in that position he commanded the stage; an able partner to Gloria Foster, herself no small force on the boards. When Clayton called to tell me Bob was dead it was so early in the epidemic we didn't even know that was what we'd come to call it. It seemed like an isolated, terrifying disaster. He'd been luminescent, an embodiment of the brilliant talent we each hoped we ourselves possessed.

Since then the grim roll call has grown too long. And again we must draw together as black people. Until recently men of color were barred from participating in the testing programs that utilized experimental medications. And although women of color are the fastest-growing group in the U.S. contracting the AIDS virus, many of the symptoms that women specifically exhibit have not been officially accepted as indicators of AIDS, leaving them with inadequate health care. So that in the horror of disease, just as in the horrors of war and poverty, African Americans as well as other people of color are left out in the open, unprovided for.

I was a speaker at the Gay Pride rally in Central Park when the New York section of the AIDS quilt was dedicated, and I walked the carefully laid out rows where quilt workers had strategically placed the needed boxes of tissue. The beautifully crafted quilt panels went on for what seemed like acres and my brothers were there—the photos, the Kente cloth, the snap queen accessories embroidered in red, black, and green. And it seemed too cruel to try and squeeze our wondrous survival of the Middle Passage, slavery, Jim Crow, and benign neglect into such a small square of fabric.

I think it is fitting that a womanly art—quilting—has come to embody a memorial instigated largely by gay men. When we try to discern what "gay" culture is, it is often found in the combination of things that highlight an irony or a difficult truth. When I watch the few popular media depictions of black lesbians or gay men I am disappointed with the flat acceptance of surface elements—campy mannerisms, colorful clothes, attitude, all of which fall quite short of that difficult truth.

When I look at "In Living Color" I may chuckle once or twice but for the most part the black gay characters, Blaine and Antoine, completely miss the irony of the new vision being created. The writers seem easily satisfied with their own ability to startle viewers by showing black men in funny outfits who lisp rather than drawing a real picture of a black drag queen, a truly outrageous and complex figure in our society. And never would the writers or the stars admit they might (if they ever took the chance) like these two characters they've created. Their casual contempt shows through. When my friend Dan makes over to look like Patti La-Belle he's acknowledging layers of cultural references that only begin with the feathers. He's postulating many relationships to the ideas of maleness, femaleness, and blackness. He is a black man and it is not an easy laugh.

Professor Calvin Herton, when discussing the new work of black women in this country, termed it "a dialectical composite of the unknown coming out of the known." When I see the AIDS Memorial Quilt, I perceive those layers of cultural reference, where they've come from and how they are expanded when used in this new way. The quilt is the re-viewing of traditional crafts, imbuing them with more poignant meaning. And the relationship between black gay men and lesbians is also a similar "dialectical composite." It is sisters and brothers with the long line of traditions behind us—some of them good, some bad—reconnecting with different spices in the pot.

Such a new dish is not always easy to prepare. Often the bitter aftertaste of our pasts and heterosexual expectations is too heavy. Even black men can think they're John Wayne. And a few of us mistakenly imagine we're Miss Scarlett, or even more problematic, somebody's mother. In some cases black gay men and lesbians have chosen to find no common ground and reject exploration of that which history has provided us, and U.S. culture encourages that separation. Men huddled together in front of televised football or wrapping themselves in the pursuit of the perfect dance floor are each a different side of the same attempt to exclude women from male life. And lesbians, certainly more than our straight sisters, often find it easier to reject the rejector rather than continue to knock on a closed door. More than once I've found myself ready to walk away from black gay men who cling stubbornly to male arrogance and gleefully condescend to women. Where the connection seems most easily forged is in activities that provide an opening and then a context for our caring. My reputation as an out lesbian writer and activist puts me in a fortunate position. Black gay men who know my work will assume the connection and the safety in our relationship.

Between me and other writers such as Essex Hemphill or Assotto Saint, it is the writing that provided us with a path to each other. Our passion for the use of words as a way to save our lives was a beacon that became an important frame of reference for trust and communication. The great sadness is that now with the AIDS epidemic, too often loss is that reference point.

Recently I rode with four black men from New York to Philadelphia to attend a memorial service. On the trip we joked about how black people name children, agonized over what we were writing or working on, caught each other up on gossip. It could have been almost any family trip.

At the church the black minister leading the service felt compelled (in the face of over a hundred gay people swelling his congregation) to emphasize God's forgiveness of our "sins." On the way back home each of us commented on the minister's lapses but we really were more interested in talking about our lost brother and all the family things that the minister clearly felt we had no right to. We laughed a lot on that drive back, as black people frequently do when faced with the unfaceable.

I was in college when my father was dying of cancer. On his hospital bed, Duke never lost his sense of humor or sense of humanity. He told me with a mischievous twinkle that his nurse, Walter, was the best in the hospital. The two of them kept up a stream of flirtatious patter right to the end. And my father never acted like that made either of them less a man. All that mattered was that he could still make connections with other people, and light up a room with his wit.

Twenty years later, riding home from the memorial service with my friends, I can see the same light. Duke may never have been able to envision such a ride or such company for me, but had he been there he would have laughed the loudest. And I wonder if his wit, like theirs, was one way to face the unfaceable. Cocooned in the gentle ride of the rental car, the sweet sound of their voices, the ribald laughter, the scent of aftershave lotion were like the sensuous music of Billie Holiday and John Coltrane that I'd learned to love while tending to my father's records. These men were comforting and familiar, like the expansive clink of my father's pocket change.

However

You Come to Me

NTOZAKE SHANGE

Ntozake Shange delivers the "four-one-one," the "here and now" from the front lines of the battle between the sexes. "Whose universe is this?" "Whose pussy is this?" are the questions that REALLY activate male/female relationships, Shange wittily muses.

The contradictions, the sometimes Byzantine contrariness of the male species, are the source of the delicious tension that produces nights made virtually cosmic by having "the world's greatest sex" as well as angry vows of celibacy sworn to girlfriends who know where you've been.

While men and women DO "live" in different worlds, Shange concludes we all hold on to our passports.

I have not entered a relationship with any man in the last twenty years in which I did not fully expect to blow to smithereens the myth of phallocentrism that buoys the dismal personal prospects of women snared by the guy on the white horse. I confess that few of my consorts were toppled from the patriarchal thrones of their imaginations, but I am certain that the volatility of most of my relationships with English-speaking African-American men can be attributed to intense ontological struggles: whose universe is this?

Ever the optimist, I set up households with a number of fellas, only to discover that: 1) If we are both artists, his work comes first and laundry and dinner are my responsibility; 2) If I am doing fairly well in my profession, this is construed as an affront of some kind that must be acted out with continued references to my good luck; 3) Differences of opinion on esthetic, political, or philosophical matters are invalid because I just don't know what I am talking about. These are all common, sometimes comical, defenses of relationships that institutions like marriage or cohabitation enforce to sustain the male entity like the Federal Reserve assists the economy. Having been referred to as money in the bank more than once, I can assure you it is not a compliment.

Alas, on this planet the nexus of women as money, women as property, women as entertainment, has not yet been dissolved. So, no matter how much we work against it or attempt to free our particular relationships from it, we are functioning in societies that require our diminution at any cost to us. For decades we have known that we are in the most grave danger of being maimed or killed by men who are our lovers or husbands, not some stranger. Yet we spend years of culturally condoned inactivity dreaming about these affairs that double our chances to die violently. They've done a great job, here, on us and our daughters. Still, I have not opted for lesbian separatism or celibacy as a lifelong avocation. Why not?

I like men.

They're sexy, funny, exciting. They've got hair in weird places. They can give me great pleasure: intellectually and sexually. On a fast bop or a mambo, they can spin me round so I feel I have the grace and speed of an intergalactic nymph. They can show me how to catch a ball or the problem with my left uppercut. I get a chance to pull out my evening bikinis with silver and black ostrich feathers or open crotches. My satin sheets take on the powers of monster roller coasters or southwestern hot springs. Their eyes light up at candlelit suppers at the beach, gourmet omelettes in the middle of the night. I can go on and on. The texture of their skin is different; they smell different. But the most important thing is that all this is given freely because it gives me pleasure.

I love my father and brothers: canny, wise, and benevolent patriarchs, both. Yet the men I've chosen (some have chosen me) to be integrals of my fairly stable foothold in the family of the future are wondrous eccentrics who are just as uncomfortable with the stiff-upper-lip hierarchy of masculinity as I am.

In fact, men have been of great significance in the twists and turns of my career from the beginning. I am saying this because it's important for us as women to know that there are men in this very world who want us to flourish, and who will help. What is real are friendships with extraordinary men that transcend craft and business.

But, men, poor things, would rather do without any of the above when that's possible rather than just enjoy it, because they think we function like they do. Dinner and dancing for them is a down payment on a piece of ass. A piece of pussy comes with a drive to the shore. A gift is ransom for your body, my dear, not a token of affection. That's why they say things like: "You

shouldn't have done all this for me"; "I don't celebrate birth-
days"; "All this fancy stuff don't do nothin' for me." Of course
not, it can't. If they enjoy any of the fruits of our culinary or
sensual imagination, upfront, that means they owe us: their bodies, which are the home of their penises, which are the raison
d'être for their superiority, which gives their souls the power to
reign over all creatures small and large. So the keen disappointment we feel when one of our fancies shoves the water chestnuts
around his plate like it was warmed-over spinach, or cursorily
glances at a negligee that was two weeks' salary, is not a manifesta-
tion of the foolhardiness of romance, but rather evidence that our
attempts to be special, if only to ourselves, must be stymied. Ordinary is the call of the day. There was nothing to it. Nothing is
going on of significance. It was an ordinary day. Nothing happened.

I don't like to have days of my own that are singularly nonde-
script. I take this to mean I am on spiritual retreat, which is
sometimes necessary, or I am at the beginning of a depression if I
don't do something about my state of mind. In other words, what
we may take to be genuine healthy interest in making our experiences unique or pleasurable, men experience as investments of
ransom for their attentions like we weren't there, too.

I mean, there are men who are honest enough to buy those
life-size plastic dollies with an opening where a vagina should be
that's filled with a sponge they can dampen. So we, in fact, are not
there and their experience is wholly their own. But, most men
like to actually have us there believing that our reality is sub-
sumed.

Years ago our lack of prescient actuality encouraged the hop-
in-and-out school of lovemaking, which also assumed that we as
women had taken birth control pills or used diaphrams, IUDs, or
"whatever." The "whatever" always took me aback. I tried to
imagine that I was an exotic beast that needed a "whatever" or
some Byzantine contraption that required a "whatever," but those
ideas were off the mark. "Whatever" was anything or nothing that
I had procured to protect my partner from what would inevitably

have been "my" pregnancy. Remember the sacred phrases: "Well, I thought you were using something"; "Weren't you using anything?" "Well, whatever."

Ordinary. Disembodied. Nameless. Pussy. Safety in nonspecificity.

My brother.

These days the language isn't quite so abstract. Most men know they should use monoxynol-treated latex condoms to save their own lives or ours, but they have very little understanding of STDs or the HIV virus. Some believe that fucking fast mitigates the virus. Others hold the belief that only sperm ejaculated into the vagina, not sperm that oozes into our mouths, is dangerous. Once again, since pussy is some independent organ *sans* female, they don't connect that women have two mouths: both are vulnerable to the implications of unprotected sex. Oh, I must not leave out the gooey eyes, the masculine set jaw and pout that accompany the guy who is accepting his fate to put a condom on; all grim and purposeful. Can it really be my fault that his sensual vocabulary is so limited, that if there's no raw penetration, this boy can't have any fun? Obviously not. But, there's even one more nonsensical than that. There are men out there who believe that lists of previous lovers extracted by interrogations, pilfering of diaries, gossip, visitations from lil' birds, can assure them of which one of us (with the pussy) is HIV-positive and which ones aren't. None of these fellas has a certifiable belief in magic, either.

As we delve further into male exotic esoterica, we must deal with the idea of male shape-shifters, though as far as I can tell it is a purely metaphorical experience. They think their penis is their fist or a celery stalk. They think our pussy is their pussy, but they're not quite sure because they continually inquire: "Who's pussy is this?" Sometimes they do this with great alarm and ferocity in their voices. If some of us are wont to touch ourselves to enhance our own pleasure, these very same fellas may demand to know what we are doing with their nipple, their clit, their bush, which apparently were appropriated without our knowledge or consent. I, myself, never had any interest in transmogrification until I saw how exponentially content men became when they believed they had their own pussies.

One last note, however. Having the pussy has in no way refined their knowledge of what to do with one: their own or anybody else's. Although I must give credit to the one or two I know who are so adept I never doubt for a second that they are all over and through me and I know he's put that Trojan on, but I don't know when or how. Oh, it's exhilarating to be with a man who wants me, wants this together sweating and tide-rising to be seamless, uninterrupted, sweet, satisfying, and specifically what we are doing with each other: the breath and time we take to look, to gaze and giggle: good safe sex.

Black Men

Do Feel About Love

AUDREY B. CHAPMAN

This choropoem of voices closes with a prescription. Of course, the word "prescription" conjures images of ill health. So often love makes us crazy, and it can make us sick. But each of these essays has been intended as a balm. Some have stung, others soothed, all read closely can heal.

Therapist Audrey B. Chapman in her practice acts as umpire, referee, and catalyst for change in the turbulent love zone her clients navigate. Chapman is witness to the under- and inside of men's souls women swear they would give anything to touch. But could we? Would we bear and accept our men stripped, trembling before our eyes? Sure we want our men to cry, just not on OUR shoulders.

Creating the space and the way to love, Chapman has found, confounds, obsesses men's energies, renders them heartbroken and speechless TOO. Women have no monopoly on right, or righteousness, in love.

The Black male style of loving, often maddening and incomprehensible to women, is complex and highly ritualized. If we require that men honor our style, we must attempt to understand theirs. Chapman allows us to see how men see us loving them, how they hear and feel our needs.

The psychological world of black men is in many ways a closed society: no women allowed. Through years of conditioning, black men have learned to keep their feelings and innermost fears to themselves. Opening up to women is too risky, black men tell me. They can't chance the sting of rejection or the uncertainty of vulnerability, because these feelings tear at the core of their sense of masculinity. Yet, in my role as therapist, I am often allowed inside the closed world of black men, and the revelations have been no less than astounding. What I have learned reinforces something I have always known—that being a black man in this society is one of the most difficult tasks anyone must face. Black women often forget this reality or too quickly dismiss it.

Black women ask me constantly why black men behave in ways which make relations with them so often acrimonious and unfulfilling. Black men ask me the same questions about black women. Why are they so domineering and controlling? Neither sex understands the behavior of the other. Consequently, we fight through many unresolved issues on whatever ground we happen to meet. Nowhere, however, is the conflict more evident than in our love relations. Sisters tell me that they are tired of hearing excuses from black men about their behavior, and they want them to shape up and do it now. Unfortunately, it just isn't that simple —not for men who will not examine themselves, feel, or show emotion.

Why can't he love me? This has become the modern black woman's lament. What I want to cry out to all black women is that he is dying to love you but he has great difficulty for a very simple reason. HE IS AFRAID! Fear, more than any other emotion, is what I believe rules the hearts and minds of many black men. So, what are they afraid of?

They are fearful of black women for many reasons. On some level, I believe they see us as collaborators with this societal system which is so hostile to their goals and aspirations. No matter how misguided this thinking may be, we need to understand why it is so. Black men believe we are less apt to fall through the fissures created by racism, and they feel that white society is more accepting of us. But the actual experience of black women past and present is one that joins us with our men in the awfulness of racism and oppression.

Black men can not easily love a black woman when they are so unsure of their commitment and loyalty. The hostility that black men receive from the larger society is displaced at home, in their relationships with women and each other. What then gets played out is a dangerous game of "I'll get them before they get me," and I see black men acting out this scenario many times over. Black men make us a target of their rage instead of striking out at the real enemies.

Black men go to great lengths to appear in control, and would die before they would admit how their fear of us controls them. I continue to be amazed at some of the truly silly situations which can arise when this fear gets a grip on them. I remember a recent conference I attended where participants were flocking to a popular session on black male/female relationships. Many of the black women arrived early and began to fill the conference room. I saw grown men stop at the door and hesitate before entering. They discussed among themselves whether they should go in when they saw so many black women. The scene was reminiscent of one from the movie *Jungle Fever,* when the men stayed outside the home because the women were inside meeting as a "war council." I overheard one brother say to another that he would not go in because "it looks like a lynching to me."

The reference to lynching surprised me. Here black women

were being linked with a heinous act of terrorism perpetrated by gangs of white men. I realized then how prevalent still is the notion among black men of the castrating black female. If this image is etched in a black man's mind, he will see its embodiment in every black woman he encounters. He will feel deep within that he has to protect himself in any way he can. The protection, though, is mostly veneer; a surface coating of cool and macho behavior, proving to the world and his woman that he is in control. What he is really saying, though, ladies, is just the opposite. What he wants to say is please love me and don't leave me, but he can't.

A black woman's anger is almost paralyzing for their men; they will take most any action to avoid it. Dr. Frank Pittman, a psychologist, writing in *Psychology Today,* states, "I don't think it off the wall to speculate that most of the problems between men and women are related to a man's panic in the face of a woman's anger." He was not writing of black men in particular but all men. And what I have seen in my office confirms this thought. Black men act out in the most strange and curious ways when faced with feminine anger, even if they feel in their hearts that the anger is justified. Why is this so?

With the black woman being such a dominant force in our families and communities, little black boys learn before they get very old that some black women are not to be messed with. Even if Mama wasn't fearsome, they knew black women in school or church who could make them shiver just with a stare or a particular stance. They tell me they experience a similar reaction in adult love relationships when their woman gets mad with them. The difference is that little boys have to stand there and take it, but grown men don't. They will hide out physically or emotionally, but either way the black woman gets the wrong message.

When black women see men in retreat, they immediately assume that this is a man who does not want to be involved. The antics of avoidance are often just that—antics. He may want to relate with all his heart but he can't risk exposure, because what's he to do if it doesn't work out? One fact which I have learned is that men and women experience rejection quite differently. Where a woman may cry and go off with her girlfriends licking her wounds, a man will keep all the pain bottled up inside. He will put on a face of indifference to the world to avoid the shame inside. And, we all know that emotions kept inside must get out some way, and unfortunately, the path outward is not always a constructive one. What a hurting man wants is a quick fix, and that's often where I come in.

The number of men who call in to my weekly radio show was initially very surprising to me. The fact is that on many of those nights more men call in than do women. When the station management apprised me of this statistic, the question on everyone's mind was why. Black men do not easily relate their pains and hurts to anyone, not even best friends or family members. So what I believe my show provides is an opportunity to discuss a "no-no" subject, namely feelings, while remaining safe behind the wall of anonymity provided by radio. I suspect that some even change their names or disguise their voices when they call. And, of course, the all-time favorite is when they call saying that a friend needs help with a particular question. They also are probably encouraged by hearing other men speak earnestly about their problems, and this gives them the nerve to dial the number.

What is also remarkable about some of my male callers is how lonely they sound. I get an image in my mind of guys who have spent the weekend in mainly lonely pursuits like watching sporting events on television, ducking into a movie, tinkering with their cars, or just about anything to help pass the time. Women, on the other hand, have the impression that black men are always out kicking up their heels, apparently never noticing the black men you see sitting on bar stools or in restaurants by themselves.

One of the most rewarding aspects of my radio show has been that many of my male callers follow up by calling my office for an appointment. This is often the first time that they have ever sought help from a therapist. I think they learn to trust me through the radio show and become comfortable with my continuing effort to be evenhanded, not readily taking sides with my own gender. They have heard me parcel out criticism to either sex depending upon the situation described to me, and therefore they are willing to trust me face-to-face with their feelings. Some come with their partners and others come alone to sort out feelings and define goals to change their patterns.

If there's any commonality among these men, it is their desire to connect with someone after years of frustration at not getting it right. What's amusing, though, about them is their heartfelt desire to get things settled in one session. This is, of course, amusing to anyone who has ever sought counseling, but some of them actually think that a lifetime pattern can be broken in one sitting. Careful not to wound their egos, I slowly attempt to create an atmosphere of trust so that we can begin to explore real feelings. Believe me, this is no easy task.

Black men are expert at hiding feelings, so it often takes several sessions before they will commit to the real work of therapy. The process of therapy is most difficult for black men. They resist and fight emotion in very artful ways. Patience is imperative on my part, because it is so easy to scare them off. My best chance with them is when their emotional distress is recent, because then the emotions are closer to the surface and easier to touch.

Because I am female they are ever watchful of my reactions, looking for any indication that I might attack or expose them to ridicule. Getting in touch with previous hurts and pain is so scary for black men. I am reminded of the many evenings that I sit in my office watching some of my male clients leave with tears streaming down their faces. I am careful not to say anything to them or let them know that I see, because I realize that while we may have made great progress, they still aren't ready for me, a woman, to see them cry.

Black men see crying as the ultimate affront to manhood. They have been taught since childhood that it is unacceptable, so they try never to do it no matter how they might really feel. We have no such constraint on our emotions: letting it all out is quite natural for us. So when we are faced with men who have no idea what emoting is about, we become impatient and critical.

"What's wrong with them?" black women often ask when faced with a man who can't speak about his feelings. Sometimes we make it even harder for them to talk by our reactions when they do try.

I conducted a relationship workshop once with another, male therapist, and we decided to put the men and women together to see what would happen when they faced each other with their feelings. The men sat in a small group in the center of the room and the women were in a circle around them. Without much hesitation, one man began to speak about his life and experiences with black women until one of the women stood up and took him to task for every word he had uttered. She threw out all kinds of negative epithets and became quite agitated just from his remarks. The other men, of course, after witnessing this outbreak, closed up tighter than they ever had before. Thus ended the discussion. However, when we pointed out what had happened to the women and how the men had stopped speaking after the verbal attack, they were slow to understand what we were talking about.

I have seen black women taking men apart for "falling apart" or "not being able to cope" when the men try to explain how they are feeling about a particular problem. This reaction is what most black men expect from us, so they hide true emotion as much as possible. Being seen as a chump or a punk is abhorrent to black men. They learn this early from other black men or "oldheads," as one black man called the older men in his neighborhood. He told me that when he was growing up, the men in the family made it clear to him that black women needed to be kept in check. The message he said was clear: "Keep her under control so that she can't dominate and manipulate you."

Young boys are taught by older men to strategize and get over on women. This is done because black men feel as powerless in the black community as they do in white society. They perceive black women as being in total control, and challenging this reality is not a battle they think they can win. Subterfuge then becomes the game of the day. Keeping the woman off balance by acting out or simply withholding affection is an example of the retaliatory methods black men may use against these "all-powerful" females who appear to be controlling their lives.

What these older men don't teach black boys is how to express the feelings needed to negotiate and take responsibility for the inevitable ups and downs of emotional relationships. They don't teach them how to protect themselves and still stay emotionally connected. They come to see every argument or disagreement as a threat to masculinity because the men before them experienced it the same way. Witnessing this constant push-and-pull effect between black men and women makes young boys long for emotional connection with the opposite sex without any positive model for doing so successfully. By the time they get to my office, they are frustrated and angry and very frightened of a future alone.

They come to see me as a one-woman rescue team. Some become infatuated with me and want to know all about me. They will ask me many personal questions about how I spend my time, if I have a man in my life, what I like to do on weekends. Others tell me that I remind them of someone. In one case a man told me that I reminded him of his first girlfriend. Some even want to make me a fantasy lover. You see, a fantasy lover is safe; a man can trust his feelings with her. She can't use his vulnerabilities against him. This is one reason, I believe, that men cheat on their wives. An extramarital relationship is what many men see as "a safe place for feelings." What we as black women need to learn is how to create this same feeling of safety for the men we want in our lives.

One of the benefits, I believe, for black men when they choose to work with a female therapist is that they can start to learn the management of emotional boundaries which is so hard for them in relationships. The process of transference, that is, the idealizing of the therapist, allows the man to transfer the therapeutic connection to an intimate bond with a significant other. If they can learn to feel safe with me, they sometimes feel more confident in taking a chance with another woman. A female therapist who has learned to forgive the men in her own life can guide male clients

toward the balance they need to learn between bonding and pres-
ervation of self. This process can become quite powerful for the
male client who never resolved these issues of boundaries with his
own mother.

Black couples tell me all the time that what their relationship
desperately needs is effective communication. However, when I
talk to the individuals, I hear that black men don't talk and that
black women don't listen. Black women would be shocked at
how many men tell me that black women just don't know how to
listen. The problem is that many black women see the kind of
listening black men want as mothering. And as one black woman
recently told me, she's "sick and tired of taking care of black
men." The intense purposeful listening that black men yearn for
has gotten confused by the black woman with the role of mother
—a role they don't want with any man and rightfully so.

Men even watch how we listen. They watch our body language, facial expressions, hand and feet positions; all the while
looking for any indication that the woman is not really interested
or ready to attack. If they see any movement they interpret as
disinterest or hostility, retreat is the ready response.

The other practice that makes a black man believe that his
feelings aren't safe with us is our need to share what's happening
in our life with others. Talking with friends and family about
problems is natural for women, but it is not so with men. They
tell me that they hate thinking that their pain and fears will be
shared outside the partnership. Women don't understand how
negatively this affects a man's ability to open up to them. They
want him to share with them, but fail to understand why he needs
to feel that this sharing is an exclusive arrangement. The thought
of others talking about his failings seems like condemnation to the
black man.

If black women would try to understand how dependent men
are in spite of how they may act, I believe we would be a long way
toward unraveling some of the mysteries of the black man's world.
Fear of sharing and the ambivalence about being dependent can
often cause a man to seem emotionally distant. This is a cover so

as not to appear too needy. I am often struck by how lonely some black men are. They are caught in a great internal struggle; needing love and being terrified of it. They also are deeply confused about physical and emotional love, and feel much safer with the former. This is why sexual prowess so often gets twisted up by black men with issues of power and control.

A man told me recently that black women always want to control his penis and that he was not having any of this. In a world where black men control very little, he made it clear to me that he would do anything to maintain control over his sexuality. I see black men taking this issue to extremes; going out of their way to behave badly just to prove a point. Even when some black men fail to maintain an erection, they can find a way to blame this on a black woman. Women are renowned for using sex to get back at men. What we need to realize is that black men do the same thing to us. They may withhold sex if they are angry, feigning headaches, fatigue, and some even begin to experience premature ejaculation. They may even stay away from us all together so they don't have to perform sexually. This is what I call "groin-level" control. It's an attempt to control the outside when the inside is in turmoil.

We have to understand that in a society where black men are denied the accoutrements of success which white men take for granted, they grope for other areas in which to exert their sense of power. Sex is the natural area to choose because society gives the black man permission to be a stud while it gives him little room to be anything else. Black men who collect women, brag about sexual marathons, and make flashy efforts at dressing and dancing seductively may seem like the most confident of men. If allowed to peek beneath all the surface bravado, you would most likely find a scared and lonely person. He acts the way he does because he knows no other way.

If I could stress only one issue with black women, it would be the necessity of understanding and accepting the fragility of our men's psyche. They desire and need bonding as much as we do, but they need a road map to get where they long to be. We have to encourage those willing to struggle with their emotions, and become more comfortable showing gentleness in the face of weakness. And when we finally meet a man who is willing to open up to us, we have to learn to listen and be patient and not tell him what he's feeling or thinking.

If black women are really tired of carrying the load in the black community, we are going to have to express to our men a willingness to share power. This can not be a halfhearted effort; we have to trust him to do what he says he can manage, which may be different from what we might expect him to do. First and foremost, we cannot mother men as we do our children. If we feel like we are taking care of a baby, we are going about it the wrong way. Men may complain about women who force them to confront their feelings, but believe me, they secretly hold disdain for those women who are compliant and submissive in the face of behavior both know is wrong.

Black women also need to learn that the hard work which accompanies self-discovery must be done by black men for themselves. We need to work on our own issues and stop spending endless hours trying to "catch a man" or "hold a man." I see too many black women who tell me they are working on a man to the detriment of their own health and welfare. This does no one any good. Black men desperately want connections. When they can find a way to cope with their many fears about us, they do, believe it or not, merge positively with black women. The prescription I urge for black women is that they learn to accept the black man's need for space to find himself and balance this need with her desire to feel adored and affirmed. This cannot happen until we learn to identify with and understand his struggle, while attending to our own.

Notes on the Contributors

TINA MCELROY ANSA is the author of the novel *Baby of the Family*, which was named a Notable Book of the Year in 1989 by the *New York Times Book Review*. Her short stories and fiction have been widely anthologized, and her journalism has appeared in the *New York Times*, the *Los Angeles Times, Newsday*, and many other newspapers. She and her husband, filmmaker Jonee' Ansa, live on St. Simons Island, Georgia.

DORISJEAN AUSTIN is the author of the novel *After the Garden*. Her work has appeared in *The Amsterdam News, The City Sun, Essence, Ms.*, and the *New York Times Book Review*. A cofounder and executive director of New Renaissance Writers, Inc., a Harlem-based writers' workshop, Ms. Austin currently teaches fiction-writing workshops at Columbia University's School of Writing, and fiction and journalism at the Frederick Douglass Creative Arts Center. Ms. Austin lives in Brooklyn, New York, and is working on her second novel.

BEBE MOORE CAMPBELL is the author of *Sweet Summer: Growing Up With and Without My Dad; Successful Women, Angry Men, Backlash in the Two-Career Marriage;* and the novel *Your Blues Ain't Like Mine*. A contributing editor of *Essence*, Ms. Campbell has written as well for *Ms., Working Mother, Ebony*, the *New York Times Magazine*, the *Washington Post, Seventeen, Parents*, and *Glamour*. She is a regular commentator for "Morning Edition" on National Public Radio, and lives in Los Angeles with her husband, daughter, and stepson.

AUDREY B. CHAPMAN is a family and marriage therapist and nationally known human relations trainer. She is the author of the books *Man Sharing: Dilemma or Choice* and *Black Men and Women: The Battle for Love and Power.* The host of her own radio talk show, "Relating," on WHUR in Washington, D.C., Ms. Chapman lectures nationally on "Male/Female Relationship Issues."

MIRIAM DECOSTA-WILLIS is a professor of African American Studies at the University of Maryland—Baltimore County. She edited *Blacks in Hispanic Literature* and the forthcoming *The Memphis Diary of Ida B. Wells.* She coedited *Erotique Noir/Black Erotica, Double Stitch: Black Women Write About Mothers and Daughters,* and *Homespun Images: An Anthology of Black Memphis Writers and Artists.*

AUDREY EDWARDS, editor-at-large for *Essence* magazine, has been a magazine editor for over fifteen years. She has been an executive editor at *Black Enterprise* and *Essence,* a senior editor at *Family Circle,* and an associate editor at *Redbook.* She is the coauthor, with Dr. Craig K. Polite, of *Children of the Dream: The Psychology of Black Success.*

PATRICE GAINES is a reporter for the *Washington Post.* She is the mother of a twenty-four-year-old daughter, Andrea Carter. Her autobiography is scheduled for publication in the spring of 1994.

MARCIA ANN GILLESPIE, the former editor in chief of *Essence* magazine, is a contributing editor of *Ms.* magazine.

MARITA GOLDEN is the author of the autobiography *Migrations of the Heart* and the novels *A Woman's Place, Long Distance Life,* and *And Do Remember Me.* She is on the faculty of the MFA Graduate Program in Creative Writing at George Mason University in Fairfax, Virginia.

JEWELLE GOMEZ is the author of two collections of poetry and a novel, *The Gilda Stories.* She is also the director of the Literature Program of the New York State Council on the Arts and frequently contributes to *Ms., The Village Voice,* and *Out/Look.* Originally from Boston, she has lived in New York since 1971.

AUDRE LORDE was the author of thirteen books of poetry and prose. Her collections of poetry include *Our Dead Behind Us, The Black Unicorn,* and *From a Land Where Other People Live,* which was nominated for a National Book Award. *The Cancer Journals,* a diary of her battle against the disease, and her "biomythography," *Zami: A New Spelling of My Name,* are among her most influential and well-known prose works. Audre Lorde lectured widely, nationally and internationally, on lesbian and gay rights, sexual, political, racial, and economic oppression. She taught and held distinguished professorships at a variety of colleges and universities, including Hunter College in New York City.

SONIA SANCHEZ is a poet, mother, activist, and professor, as well as a national and international lecturer on Black culture and literature, women's liberation, peace, and racial justice. She is the author of thirteen books, including *I've Been a Woman: New and Selected Poems, Homegirls and Handgrenades,* and most recently, *Under a Soprano Sky.* Sonia Sanchez has received awards from the National Endowment for the Arts, and she holds the Laura Carnell Chair in English at Temple University.

KESHO YVONNE SCOTT teaches American studies and sociology at Grinnell College in Grinnell, Iowa. In addition to *The Habit of Surviving: Black Women's Strategies for Life,* she is the coauthor of *Tight Spaces,* winner of an American Book Award.

NTOZAKE SHANGE, playwright, poet, novelist, actress, is the author of the highly acclaimed, award-winning play, *for colored girls who have considered suicide when the rainbow is enuf.* Her novels include *Sassafras, Cypress & Indigo,* and *Betsey Brown.* She is the author of numerous collections of poetry, among them *Nappy Edges* and *A Daughter's Geography.* Her theater productions include *Spell #7* and an adaptation of Bertolt Brecht's *Mother Courage and Her Children.*

JUDY DOTHARD SIMMONS has been an editor and writer for more than twenty years with *Essence, Black Enterprise, Emerge,* and many other national magazines. Her latest volume of poetry was published by Blind Beggar Press in the Bronx, New York. Currently, she is a columnist and editor with the *Anniston Star* in Anniston, Alabama.

Acknowledgments

ANSA: "A New Shower Massage, Phone Sex, and Separation" copyright © 1993 by Tina McElroy Ansa. Printed by permission of the author.

AUSTIN: "The Act Behind the Word" originally appeared as "The Thirty Year Rape" in *Essence* magazine, January 1991, vol. 21, no. 9. Copyright © 1991 by DorisJean Austin. Reprinted by permission of the author.

CAMPBELL: "Black Men, White Women: A Sister Relinquishes Her Anger" copyright © 1993 by Bebe Moore Campbell. Printed by permission of the author.

CHAPMAN: "Black Men Do Feel About Love" copyright © 1993 by Audrey B. Chapman. Printed by permission of the author.

DECOSTA-WILLIS: "Letting Go with Love" copyright © 1993 by Miriam DeCosta-Willis. Printed by permission of the author.

EDWARDS: "Sleeping with the Enemy" copyright © 1993 by Audrey Edwards. Printed by permission of the author.

GAINES: "Tough Boyz and Trouble: Those Girls Waiting Outside D.C. Jail Remind Me of Myself" first appeared in the *Washington Post*, February 23, 1992. Copyright © 1992 by the *Washington Post*. Reprinted by permission of the *Washington Post*.

GILLESPIE: "Delusions of Safety: A Personal Story" first appeared in *Ms.* magazine, September/October 1990, vol. 1, no. 2. Copyright © 1990 by Marcia A. Gillespie. Reprinted by permission of the author.

GOLDEN: "Walking in My Mother's Footsteps to Love" copyright © 1993 by Marita Golden. Reprinted by permission of the author.

GOMEZ: "In the Wink of an Eye: Black Lesbians and Gay Men Together" copyright © 1993 by J. L. Gomez. Printed by permission of the author.